MAKING ENGLISH LAND⌐ CHANGING PERSPECTIVES

*Papers presented to Christopher Taylor
at a symposium held at Bournemouth University
on 25th March 1995*

Edited by

Katherine Barker and Timothy Darvill

Bournemouth University
School of Conservation Sciences
Occasional Paper 3

Oxbow Monograph 93
1997

Published by Oxbow Books
Park End Place
Oxford OX1 1HN

Tel: 01865-241249
Fax: 01865-754449

ISBN 1 900188 50 3

School of Conservation Sciences
Bournemouth University
Occasional Paper 3

ISSN 132 – 6094

Front cover: Agglestone, Studland, Dorset [photograph: Timothy Darvill].

Printed in Great Britain by The Short Run Press, Exeter

Contents

Preface

On Saturday 25th March 1995 about 200 people gathered together in Bournemouth University for a symposium entitled 'The Making of the English Landscape: Changing Perspectives'. The meeting, organized in association with the Centre for South Western Historical Studies, University of Exeter, had two main purposes. First, to celebrate the 25th anniversary of the publication of Christopher Taylor's book entitled *Dorset* in Hodder and Stoughton's *Making of the English Landscape* series. Second, to review, through recent studies by a number of well-known practitioners in the field, aspects of the way that perspectives and approaches to the historical dimensions of the landscape have changed over the past quarter-century or so.

The keynote address was given by Christopher Taylor, distinguished as the only author to contribute to two volumes to *The Making of the English Landscape* series, and it is to Christopher Taylor that this series of papers is presented.

All the papers given at the symposium are published here except one, that by Catherine Stoertz on aerial photography, which will appear elsewhere. Editorial policy has been to tamper as little as possible with the papers provided by the speakers so as to preserve something of the freshness and spontaneity that was such a welcome feature of the symposium itself.

In organizing the symposium, and in preparing these papers, the editors are very grateful to Christopher Taylor and to all the other speakers who gladly gave of their time and effort. There were a number of people who, unable to contribute through age or other commitments, sent their warmest good wishes. We would especially like to thank Professor Bryan Brown, Head of the School of Conservation Sciences, for his help and encouragement throughout, and for his words of welcome to participants at the symposium; and also Alan Hunt, Chris Morgan, Adrian Murray, Louise Pearson, Andy Fulton, Nicola King and Kate Macdonald for their assistance and help in various ways.

The symposium was very pleased to welcome Margaret Body, Senior Editor at Hodder and Stoughton, whose note of appreciation follows this Preface.

Katherine Barker and Timothy Darvill
Bournemouth
January 1997

List of contributors

Katherine Barker. Senior Lecturer in Continuing Education. School of Conservation Sciences, Bournemouth University, Fern Barrow, Poole, Dorset BH12 5BB

Margaret Body. Senior Editor, Hodder and Stoughton, 47 Bedford Square, London WC1B 3DP

Timothy Darvill. Professor of Archaeology. School of Conservation Sciences, Bournemouth University, Fern Barrow, Poole, Dorset BH12 5BB

Peter Fowler. Emeritus Professor of Archaeology. Department of Archaeology, University of Newcastle, Newcastle upon Tyne, Tyne and Wear NE1 7RU

Peter Herring. Senior Archaeologist. Cornwall Archaeological Unit, Cornwall County Council, Old County Hall, Station Road, Truro, Cornwall TR1 3AY

Dr Robert Higham. Senior Lecturer. Department of History and Archaeology, University of Exeter, The Queen's Building, Queen's Drive, Exeter EX4 4QH

Dr Della Hooke. Senior Lecturer. Department of Geography and Geology, Cheltenham and Gloucester College of Further Education, Francis Close Hall, Swindon Road, Cheltenham, Gloucestershire GL50 4AZ

Nicholas Johnson. County Archaeologist for Cornwall. Cornwall Archaeological Unit, Cornwall County Council, Old County Hall, Station Road, Truro, Cornwall TR1 3AY

Christopher Taylor. 13 West End, Whittlesford, Cambridge, Cambridgeshire CB2 4LX

Dr Tom Williamson. Senior Lecturer. Centre for East Anglian Studies, University of East Anglia, Norwich, Norfolk NR4 7TJ

A note of appreciation

Margaret Body

Publishing W G Hoskins' *The Making of the English Landscape* and the county series that blossomed from it on a non-academic publishing list was a conscious decision which called for some expertise in tightrope-walking. The series had various manifestations between the 1950s and late 1980s before eventually it fell off the tightrope. W G Hoskins himself of course knew exactly how to talk to the general public, as his later TV career testified. And of the other tightrope walkers, quite the most able was Chris Taylor whose *Dorset* in 1970 was one of the two volumes which launched the second and most flourishing period for the county by county series.

Chris Taylor not only knew how to communicate his academic enthusiasm to the wider market but was that thing cherished by publishers' editors, a thoroughly professional author. He has the distinction of being the only author who contributed a second volume to the series. (We angled for a third without success). His *Dorset* and *Cambridgeshire* volumes are among the best in *The Making of the English Landscape* series and so it was a particular pleasure to attend the symposium to mark the 25th anniversary of *Dorset*'s publication, to enjoy the diversity of his peers, to hear Chris himself elegantly itemizing *Dorset*'s current limitations, as academics who have not stood still for 25 years will tend to do, and to think that it was a damn fine book for all that.

1   Introduction: Landscape old and new

Katherine Barker and Timothy Darvill

Landscapes are not what they used to be. Naturally. Both physically and intellectually, that entity which is known as landscape is always changing and will continue to do so. Today the study of contemporary landscapes, and the understanding of ancient ones, is at the forefront of so much archaeological research in Britain and abroad. But it was not always so.

Landscape Archaeology is a relatively new field of inquiry. It initially grew from a number of academic traditions, perhaps most particularly the field of geography (Aston and Rowley 1974, 11–12), but history is strongly implicated too. In 1957 Maurice Beresford selected the title *History on the Ground* for a collection of six case studies in maps and landscapes at a time when archaeology was more often thought of in terms of history under the ground, and even then usually monument- or site-based.

The development of Landscape Archaeology has run parallel to, and is often considered interchangeable with, what is called Landscape History. True to its roots, the whole field of landscape studies is remarkably eclectic and outward-looking with many insights derived from other disciplines, notably historical geography, sociology, history of art, literature and environmental science, not forgetting the most recent arrival on the academic scene, heritage management. It is perhaps because of this multi-disciplinary interest in a common phenomenon that the word 'landscape' has made its way into almost every corner of everyday life. In one sense such diversity has served to obscure the objectives of landscape studies, but at the same time it has focused attention on the common raw material with which everyone in the field is working. Landscape History does not have a single theoretical perspective or set of approaches, how can it? As Christopher Taylor observes later in this book, Landscape History is:

> not archaeology, nor local history, not architectural history nor geography ... not just the fitting of documentary history into a physical or spatial setting ... nor is it merely looking at maps and air photographs and noting significant patterns. It is all these and more. The landscape is a primary source of evidence which we have to learn how to read. (Taylor this volume, 11)

From source to first new understandings

The papers in this volume are all landscape studies in the general sense, but each develops and illustrates a particular approach or set of perspectives, drawing on selected facets of the raw data or using specific theoretical models. It is appropriate to start, however, with the common ancestor to so many studies of the English landscape: William George Hoskins, Hatton Professor of English History at Leicester 1965–68.

In Hoskins' early career we see something of the influences that moulded his distinctive approach. In 1948 he became first Reader in English Local History at Leicester, whence he moved to Oxford in 1951 as Reader in Economic History. Hoskins belonged to that rather special generation of scholars whose life and works straddled the Second World War with all the hardship, misery, intensity of feeling and, in a sense, opportunity that flowed from it. Hoskins belonged to a generation nurtured on O G S Crawford's field archaeology, H C Darby's historical geography, A Clapham's economic history and the results of systematic aerial reconnaissance of the landscape through not one but two World Wars. This last-mentioned influence is especially important. The impact of twentieth-century war on the development of air photography and its conceptual legacy is one that cannot be underestimated (Wilson 1982, 10–15). As Bradford notes:

> During the last War topographical work in an unparalleled variety of landscapes demanded rigorous standards and the exercise of controlled imagination ... [the result of which is that] discovery in archaeology ... is accelerating every year ... archaeology's progress in charting human history is no small matter; a particularly important development is the increased emphasis on piecing together social units ... as contrasted with the continual sampling of sites. Archaeology has a dual role to play regionally, making comparisons in space and also in time ... [the] total mapping of ancient landscapes ... is the latest expression, on a larger scale, of the policy which General Pitt-Rivers inaugurated in excavation. (Bradford 1957, vii–viii).

It was the publication in 1955 of Hoskins' *The Making of the English Landscape* that broke new ground in drawing these disparate but interconnected threads together under an immediately appealing title. All the ingredients were there: attention to the survival and interpretation of features preserved in the countryside, the spatial dimensions imported from geography, interpretations grounded in economic and social history and the extensive use of aerial photographs.[1] The 'importance of this work in changing people's attitude to the landscape and their environment as a whole cannot be overestimated' states the programme notes of a conference held in London in 1980 to celebrate the 25th anniversary of its publication. Organized by *Archaeological Education* in association with Hodder and Stoughton, a capacity audience packed itself into the Scientific Lecture Theatre at 23 Savile Row, London.

Among this London audience was the ghost-writer for Jennifer Aldridge and John Tregorran, fictional joint authors of a consummately skilful piece of writing (inspired by BBC Radio 4's long-running soap *The Archers*) which described the making of the Ambridge landscape, published under the title *Ambridge: An English Village Through the Ages* (Aldridge and Tregorran 1981). Perhaps more than anything else, this little book shows the widespread impact that the whole academic and literary genre of landscape studies had achieved by the early 1980s.

The value, and potential widespread appeal, of real detailed, regionally-based, studies of the landscape can be seen in the county-based volumes published by Hodder and Stoughton in a series also known as *The Making of the English Landscape*. Under the general editorship of W G Hoskins (latterly with the assistance of Roy Millward), the first to be produced was for Cornwall, published in 1955 (Balchin 1955). The Dorset volume, written by Christopher Taylor, was published in 1970.

Hoskins' work and his contribution to landscape studies in particular has been reviewed several times (e.g. Meinig 1979; Taylor 1980; Aston 1983). But one of the greatest achievements of *The Making of the English Landscape* itself and the regional histories that developed from it, is the degree to which, 40 years on, it can still be seen as the pioneering work Hoskins himself modestly claimed it to be:

> Despite the multitude of books about English landscape and scenery ... there is not one book which deals with the historical evolution of the landscape as we know it. The result is a new kind of history ... *The Making of the English Landscape* is a pioneer study, in which one has to feel one's way all the time ... I hope that individual books on the counties will help ... take us nearer to the exact truth of the way in which things happened. (Hoskins 1955, 13–15)

The fact that we can never arrive at an 'exact truth' in history (or in anything else for that matter) does not detract one jot from the excitement of being shown another way of looking for it. As Taylor once put it, Hoskins' book 'remains a milestone in the study of history, a brilliant exercise in methodology and an exquisitely written account of the development of the English landscape' (Hoskins 1988, 7).

The seminal quality of Hoskins' work lies in the establishment of landscape history as a new and proper branch of history, a way of thinking that has grown into an acknowledged discipline to the extent that it is now difficult to reconstruct the 'mind-set' of the time before such insights were available. We live in an age where an evolutionary approach is highly relevant. Study of landscape evolution bestows a corresponding sense of order, a meaning and validity to one area of human experience that now forms an essential part of the whole environmental canon.

But just as the landscape is never static, neither are interpretations and understandings of it. In 1973 Hoskins wrote that 'I became aware as I continued my explorations ... that I had not thought of all the possible questions, let alone given all the answers.' (1973, 5). The problem, of course, is all about recognizing what is significant, and accepting that others see things differently. The upland moors of south-west England and elsewhere provide an excellent example of this kind of changing perspective. In 1955 Hoskins wrote:

> The oldest recognisable cornfields, small irregular plots of ground associated with hut circles on the western side of Dartmoor, date possibly from the early Bronze Age. There are others on the western slopes of Rough Tor on Bodmin Moor in Cornwall, and similar sites with small curvilinear plots have been found on the Yorkshire Moors where they are attributed to the middle Bronze Age. These prehistoric fields are, however,

> recognisable to the archaeologist, and then only at certain times of the year, and they can hardly be said to be a feature of the landscape wherever they are. (Hoskins 1955, 21)

Yet it is now widely recognized that such features are quite visible, relatively easily recognizable, and do have an impact on the character of the modern countryside.

The physical remains have not grown: if anything they have decayed since Hoskins' day. It is the way we see them that has changed, and at least part of this is because of detailed archaeological investigations. When Elizabeth Gawne and John Somers Cox published their *Parallel reaves on Dartmoor* in 1968 a careful analysis of the landscape evidence drew them to the inescapable conclusion that the reave system could only be prehistoric in origin, as Hoskins' and others had contended. But the paper attracted little attention. It was Andrew Fleming's work that demonstrated the veracity of the claim while at the same time creating a class of landscape monument to which the reaves belonged – the coaxial field system – and giving them a European context (Fleming 1984; 1988).

The need to take stock regularly of what is known of a landscape is critically important. In Chapter 2 of this book Christopher Taylor takes up the challenge by looking back with a critical eye over his book *Dorset* in *The Making of the English Landscape* series.

Taking landscapes to the public

As we have already suggested, public interest in the idea of landscapes in general and specific areas of landscape in particular is well established in England. Over recent decades there has been no lack of recruits in pursuit of that particular variety of 'exact truth' of which Hoskins spoke. Indeed, the growth of landscape studies characteristic of the last few years yet continues, especially in university and college departments, in continuing and adult education and in county and local societies.

It is appropriate here to record the major part played by university extra-mural departments in fostering public interest and promoting field survey and research through adult education classes.[2] All of the speakers at the Bournemouth Symposium have at one time or another been involved with extra-mural teaching, but Christopher Taylor (Cambridge) and Peter Fowler (Bristol) are doyens in this field.

One possible reason for the success of extra-mural studies in relation to landscapes is that if there is a History (or Archaeology) for Everyman then it is often likely to be found, and visible, on our respective doorsteps; the ground plan and pattern of our everyday lives provides an academic discipline which can engage the attention of both local society member and senior scholar. Taylor (1988, 7) puts this achievement on a level with that of Macaulay and Trevelyan, this ability to reach out to, and profoundly affect, hundreds of thousands of ordinary people who would otherwise have never thought about the past.

Place-names provide a particularly good example of a feature of landscapes that on the one hand impinge on everyday life while on the other require expert knowledge to interpret. In Chapter 3 Della Hooke considers the difficulties of using place-names to understand early settlement patterns.

Place-names are also one of the many elements of the landscape which betray regional differences and regional character. In an age where rapid travel and European Treaties are shrinking the world, the importance of local identity and regional character seems to be increasing. Landscape characterization is very much part of this trend, and in Chapter 4 Peter Herring and Nicholas Johnson explain a mapping programme they have been carrying out in Cornwall.

Through landscape character mapping, historic landscape quality has now become a legal commodity that can be measured, traded and used in the name of planning. Couched in appropriate language, the Heritage Landscape has effectively arrived in Local Government. But can and should historic landscapes be created and commodified? In Chapter 5 Peter Fowler reviews the situation in Northumbria, looking at the way landscapes there have been interpreted by academics, managed and restored in various ways and, most recently, recreated as a working vision of an earlier form at Bede's World in Jarrow.

Alternative visions

'There is none so blind as he who will not see' runs the old adage, and seeing landscapes is no exception. Once something has been seen, and once others are convinced that they can see it too, then it enters the realm of the obvious from whence it can be endlessly disputed but never wholly ignored. The work of Hoskins, and the essentially evolutionary and positivist approach he advocated, has dominated landscape studies for more than three decades. Yet this was not the only approach to landscape being pursued in the 1950s, and it is therefore not surprising that other theoretical perspectives are now being explored in more detail and with profit.

From the early 1990s work in the field of social archaeology, itself drawing inspiration from the field of cultural geography, has played an important role, mainly through what has come to be labelled contextualism or post-processual approaches. In this essentially humanist view, landscape provides the context for social action and is therefore socially constructed. Looking back, such views can be glimpsed running through the writings of many archaeologists, including, for example, John Bradford whose book *Ancient landscapes. Studies in Field Archaeology* (Bradford 1957) was published two years after Hoskins' *The Making of the English Landscape*. But one of the most eloquent early applications of such approaches came from the pen of Jacquetta Hawkes in her evocative book *A Land*. A short extract exemplifies the whole:

> Up and down the country, whether they have been set up by men, isolated by weathering or by melting ice, conspicuous stones are commonly identified with human beings. Most of our Bronze Age circles and menhirs have been thought by the country people living round them to be men and women turned to stone. The names often help to express this identification and its implied sense of kinship; Long Meg and her daughters, the Nine Maidens, the Bridestone and the Merry Maidens. It is right that they should most often be seen as women, for somewhere in the mind of everyone is an awareness of woman as earth, as rock, as matrix. (Hawkes 1951, 91–2).

Shortly after its publication, Hawkes' book was described by Harold Nicholson as 'prophetic' in a review published in the *Observer* newspaper. And prophetic perhaps it was, in the sense that it now evokes a response in a post-Hoskins generation of landscape archaeologists reared on social archaeology, anthropology and sociology instead of history and geography.

Exploring the cultural and symbolic aspects of landscape is a growing field, not only in archaeology. There are already a number of very able exponents, and their approach in relation to earlier work is well summed up by Cosgrove and Daniels in their introduction to *The Iconography of Landscape*:

> A landscape is a cultural image, a pictorial way of representing, structuring or symbolising surroundings. ... A landscape ... is more palpable but no more real, nor less imaginary, than a landscape painting or poem ... every study of landscape further transforms its meaning, depositing yet another layer of cultural meaning. In human geography the interpretation of landscape and culture has a tendency to reify landscape as an object of empiricist investigation, but its practitioners often do gesture towards landscape as cultural symbol or image, notably when likening a landscape to a text and its interpretation as 'reading'. (Cosgrove and Daniels 1988, 1)

Prehistoric archaeology is one area where post-processualist approaches find obvious application. In Chapter 6 Timothy Darvill provides a critical review of changing orientations to the matter of landscape in field archaeology and develops a case study of the area around Dorchester, Dorset, during the later Neolithic using post-processual theoretical perspectives.

However, the prehistoric past is by no means the only domain in which post-processualist approaches can be applied. In Chapter 7 Tom Williamson looks at the way in which post-medieval societies regarded the management and use of animals which were neither wild nor domesticated: what he terms intermediate forms of exploitation.

Overview

Landscape studies now represent an immense subject area to which these papers can only make a small contribution. But through these papers we see exemplified some of the most able work in the field. We see the study of the past as an exercise in curiosity and construction, one that requires a continual defining and refining of evidence, a continual synthesis and re-synthesis.

Landscape as history, as archaeology, as itself, has no words of its own. It may speak to us, it may have to be read, but we are left free to analyze the syntax, develop our own grammar and, in the end, construct our own narratives: to make our own landscapes. Perhaps more than anything else, the contrasting perspectives offered by, for example, Hawkes and Hoskins, show that the English landscape is not simply the product of people in the past, but, like all history, is an integral part of the present; something continually 'made' and 're-made' which can never be finished. In the final chapter in this book, Chapter 8, Robert Higham draws out some themes for the future.

Notes

1. 21 out of the 82 plates in the book are aerial photographs or high-level perspective drawings.
2. Even the fictional inhabitants of *The Archers*, Radio 4's long-running soap, got themselves ankle-deep in landscape history (the script writers have always been anxious to reflect real life in the countryside):

Concern for the landscape has grown rapidly in recent years, and in the autumn of 1979 Borsetshire County Council Department of Museum Services organised a series of lectures to help amateurs to study the changing landscape of their own parishes. The lectures were advertised in the Borchester Echo as part of Borchester Technical College's usual programme of evening classes, and attracted the attention of two Ambridge residents, Jennifer Aldridge of Home Farm and John Tregorran of Manor Court. Jennifer was already playing a prominent part in the local conservation movement and John had already spent many years compiling material for a history of Ambridge. They were later joined by Shula and Pat Archer, Freddie Danby and Caroline Bone.

The course of lectures started in September and ended two months later, in good time for the participants to make a start on their survey work in the winter months. Seven parishes in the Borchester area have since been mapped, but the Ambridge survey is the only one so far to be published, and its appearance is due in no small measure to the sympathy and encouragement of Jack Woolley, owner of Grey Gables Country Club and a director of the Borchester Press.

It was Mr Woolley who realised the potential interest, among a wide readership, of a book which would chart in detail the landscape history of a typical village of the English Shires ... What follows ... is the results of the landscape survey itself, carried out over 18 laborious months. (Let nobody think it is easy! An entire day plodding round the slopes of Lakey Hill or squelching along the muddy banks of the Am in February might yield only a couple of tentative lines on a sketch map). The survey covers the landscape history of the village up to the eighteenth century, and includes the identification of the site of Ambridge's deserted medieval village and the discovery of a traceried medieval window in a barn at Grange Farm. The team's efforts to trace and establish the Saxon boundaries of Ambridge and the dates of the principal woods and boundary hedges make it possible to say, with reasonable confidence, which features of the man-made landscape have survived for the past nine hundred years. (Aldridge and Tregorran 1981, 1–3).

Bibliography

Aldridge J, and Tregorran J, 1981, *Ambridge, an English Village Through the Ages*. The Borchester Press in association with Eyre Methuen

Aston, M, 1983, The Making of the English Landscape – the next 25 years. *The Local Historian*, 15.6

Aston M, and Rowley T, 1974, *Landscape Archaeology: An Introduction to Fieldwork Techniques on Post-Roman Landscapes*. Newton Abbot. David and Charles

Balchin, W G V, 1955, *Cornwall*. London. Hodder and Stoughton

Bradford, J, 1957, *Ancient Landscapes. Studies in Field Archaeology*. London. Bell and Sons

Beresford M, 1957, *History on the Ground, Six Studies in Maps and Landscapes*. London. Lutterworth Press

Cosgrove D, and Daniels S, 1988, *The Iconography of Landscape: Essays on the Symbolic Representation, Design and Use of Past Environments*. Cambridge Studies in Historical Geography. Cambridge. Cambridge University Press

Fleming A, 1984, The prehistoric landscape of Dartmoor: Wider implications. *Landscape History*, 6, 5–19

Fleming, A, 1988, *The Dartmoor Reaves*. London. Batsford

Gawne E, and Somers Cox J, 1968, Parallel Reaves on Dartmoor. *Transactions of the Devonshire Association*, 100, 277–91

Hawkes, J, 1951, *A Land*. London. Cresset Press

Hoskins, W G, 1955, *The Making of the English Landscape*. London. Hodder and Stoughton

Hoskins, W G, 1973, *English Landscapes*. London. BBC

Hoskins, W G, 1988, with a General Introduction by Christopher Taylor, *The Making of the English Landscape* (Revised edition). London. Hodder and Stoughton

Meinig, D W, 1979, Reading the landscape. An appreciation of W G Hoskins and J B Jackson. In D W Meinig (ed), *The interpretation of ordinary landcapes*. Oxford. Oxford University Press. 195–244

Taylor, C, 1970, *Dorset*. London. Hodder and Stoughton

Taylor, C, 1973, *The Cambridgeshire Landscape*. London. Hodder and Stoughton

Taylor, C, 1980, The Making of the English Landscape – 25 years on. *The Local Historian*, 14.4

Wilson, D R, 1982, *Air Photo Interpretation for Archaeologists*. London. Batsford

2   Dorset and beyond

Christopher Taylor

It is somewhat presumptuous to imply, as the above title does, that the publication of *Dorset* (Taylor 1970) almost half a lifetime ago was a major landmark in the development of landscape history. It certainly was not. It was merely an inevitable development of ideas in W G Hoskins's seminal publication *The Making of the English Landscape* (1955) which was backed up by his other works, especially *Leicestershire* (1957), as well as by Finberg's *Gloucestershire* (1955), Milward's *Lancashire* (1955), and Balchin's *Cornwall* (1955). And indeed *Dorset* did not stand alone. There were already other scholars including Beresford (1954; 1957), Thorpe (1951) and St Joseph (Beresford and St Joseph 1958) who had been working on aspects of landscape history long before either I or *Dorset* appeared on the scene. And of course the real foundations of landscape history had been laid by previous generations of scholars, especially O G S Crawford (1953) but also by others including Allcroft (1908) and Darby (1936; 1940) and, by perhaps the greatest of them all, who wrote about it almost in his spare time, Maitland (1897).

Nor at a personal level was *Dorset* the beginning of landscape history for me. My interest in it started as a child, with the luck to have a father who, had he had the opportunities which came to my generation, would have made a much better landscape historian than I ever will. It continued at the University of Keele where Professor S H Beaver and Mr (now Professor) W M Williams taught me more than I think they ever realized and at the Institute of Archaeology, London, where I was much helped by that kindest of men, Professor W F Grimes. But it was the county of Dorset and especially the people with whom I worked for the Royal Commission on the Historical Monuments of England, that really allowed me to see that landscape history was the most wonderful way of looking at the past that could be imagined. These colleagues included Peter Fowler, Desmond Bonney and the one who taught us all, Collin Bowen.

But what is this landscape history that I have spent my life working on and writing and thinking about? It is easier to say what it is not. It is not archaeology, nor local history. It is not architectural history nor geography, although it uses the techniques and results of all these disciplines. It is not merely the fitting of documentary history into a physical or spatial setting as much that purports to be landscape history seems to be. Nor is it merely looking at maps and air photographs and noting significant patterns. It is all these and more. It is primarily the study of the landscape itself; seeing and understanding all aspects of human endeavour and failure which other sources and methods may not be capable of showing, can only confirm or perhaps only hint at. The landscape is a primary source of evidence which we have to learn to read just as we read books, documents, photographs and maps.

But where does and did *Dorset* fit in to all this? For although landscape history was only in its infancy when I wrote *Dorset*, in the time since it appeared, and there is certainly no connection, landscape history has grown up and become a respectable discipline. Here I would like to examine how various ideas and concepts current in landscape history in the 1960s have changed in the ensuing years by looking at *Dorset*.

Looking back, I am surprised how well *Dorset* has worn. It was the first book I wrote and thus has all the overconfidence and brashness of intellectual immaturity. And there are of course yawning gaps in it, mainly due to ignorance, but also because many of the basic problems of the landscape were only then beginning to be addressed. Being county-based, it also failed to use, make or understand wider connections or relationships.

So, my lack of knowledge of architectural history meant that I failed dismally to appreciate some of the important buildings of the county. Although it was mentioned, I did not see the significance of Kingston Lacy as a house designed by Pratt (Gunther 1928; RCHME 1975, Pamphill [4]) and thus its place in the development of both architectural style and living arrangements. The perhaps less important, still significant and certainly more beautiful house at Chettle by Archer also passed me by (Whiffen 1950; RCHME 1972, Chettle [2]).

Other aspects of the county's landscape were ignored because I was too young or too close to the events which created them and so did not see their historical significance. Thus the wonderful South Bridge at Wareham of 1927 in an interesting sub-Art Deco style was ignored. More importantly the Second World War, which I had lived through, was not regarded as history at all. So the place of the radar towers at Ringstead and the airfield at Warmwell in the history of the air defence system of this country was missed, as was the importance of Tarrant Rushton airfield for airborne warfare and the traces of the temporary military hospital in Kingston Lacy park (Ashworth 1986).

But despite these enormities, and many others which I shall not disclose, *Dorset* has not only stood the test of time but can now be read to see what developed from and alongside it, both at a personal level and in a wider national setting. For implicitly or explicitly, most of the problems in understanding the making of the English landscape, which have long bothered historians, and many of which still remain unsolved, were touched upon to some degree in *Dorset*.

Before the Saxons

One of the most important aspects of the Dorset landscape which I tried to emphasize was the relevance of the prehistoric and Roman landscapes to the later ones. This may seem obvious now, but in the late 1960s when I wrote *Dorset*, landscape history began with the arrival of the Saxons. It was assumed that these people chopped their way through impenetrable forests, sailed up navigable, and often clearly unnavigable, rivers to find delightfully situated spring-lines, well-mown gravel patches or neatly signposted fords. Here they could settle, arrange their new houses around a green or carefully align them along a road and then set off to democratically lay out their open fields in the newly reclaimed surrounding land (Hoskins 1955, 38).

Prehistorians, who in any case at that time did not come into landscape history, themselves toiled in primeval forests, studying the remains of people who had laid trails of axes or spearheads across the land to mark their paths (Fox 1952). The Neolithic period began on the dot of 2000 BC (Piggott 1954), virtually nothing except burial mounds marked the Bronze Age countryside and the Iron Age was limited to a few centuries when a handful of people, normally labelled A, B or C, but sometimes A/B, sat tight in well defended hillforts (Hawkes 1959). This may be amusing to a younger generation, but it was what I was taught in the late 1950s at a foremost university department for British prehistory. Even the Romans were seen as occupying little more than a few major villas, themselves within the all-pervading woodland, except on the downlands and in the eastern fens, where the lack of villas clearly indicated great imperial estates (Collingwood and Myres 1936, 27–31 and 222–3; Richmond 1955, 109–48; Taylor 1967c).

In writing *Dorset* I tried to indicate some of the more obvious features which made such interpretations impossible. I pointed not only to the large number of later prehistoric and Roman settlements, on both uplands and lowlands, on heavy land as well as on light soils but also to the field systems and the linking trackways that by then were being identified. I suggested that the ubiquitous Bronze Age round barrows might actually indicate where the missing settlements of the period were. I also began to point out that the imbalance between the numbers of sites on high land when compared with the lack of them in the lowlands might have had something to do with later destruction and land use (Taylor 1972a). Knowlton Rings close to the River Allen and the wonderfully evocative and certainly low-lying Poor Lot Barrow Group in Winterborne Abbas are among the numerous examples of lowland survival which gave the game away (RCHME 1970a, 460–3; 1975, Woodlands [19–60]).

But at the same time I was as myopic as any of my contemporaries in my inability to see beyond old ideas and concepts. I described in some detail, although thankfully did not name it, the Deverel-Rimbury culture. During my time in Dorset, Collin Bowen, who is probably the finest field archaeologist of this century, had not only recorded the thousands of acres of prehistoric fields which then existed in the county, but had recognized for the first time the great spreads of these fields which had been laid out across the landscape with no regard to the underlying topography (RCHME 1970b, Ancient Field Group 45). These were the first examples found of planned prehistoric landscapes which were later to be discovered on Dartmoor, along the River Trent and elsewhere (Rodwell 1978; Drury and Rodwell 1980; Riley 1980; Williamson 1986a; Fleming 1988; Whimster 1989). Yet I failed altogether to see the significance of these fields in terms of the development of the landscape.

Since those early days historians of the prehistoric and Roman landscapes have provided confirmation from all over England and especially from Dorset of my hesitant guesses about the density of pre-Saxon settlement (Taylor 1975; Bradley 1978; Wainwright 1979; Mercer 1981; Fowler 1983; Williamson 1984 and 1986b; Frere 1987; Ross 1987; Sunter and Woodward 1987; Addison 1989; Moore and Ross 1989; Fulford 1990; Barrett *et al.* 1991a and 1991b; Cox and Hearne 1991; Salway 1981; Sharples 1991; Woodward 1991; Lucas 1993; Hall and Coles 1994). Their work has been aided by evidence from developments in palaeobotany, dating techniques, aerial photography and most of all by excavations on a scale and in numbers undreamed of 25 years ago. So the true significance of prehistoric and Roman people in establishing not only the foundations but also the basic framework of the English landscape is now properly appreciated.

Continuity

A major theme which I discussed in *Dorset* yet which has still not been satisfactorily settled was the matter of continuity from late Roman to early Saxon times. Like most scholars in the late 1960s I had a very simplistic view of the Saxon invasions. *Dorset* even had a wonderfully archaic map with large curving arrows marking the lines of approach by the incoming Saxons. But I was then, and still am, concerned as to what exactly was transferred from the Romans to the Saxons and more importantly how the landscape was affected. Was there continuity of population, tenure, religion or political organization? In writing *Dorset* I concentrated on population and tenure as being the most significant aspects in terms of landscape. I still think this was probably correct although I now think that all four aspects continued through into Saxon times.

Since the 1960s much work has been carried out on this problem within the county and beyond, but it remains one of the most controversial and unresolved questions of landscape history (Bonney 1966 and 1976; Ford 1976; Hooke 1982; Arnold 1984; Everitt 1986). In recent papers Bruce Eagles and Patrick Hase have pulled together the limited amount of archaeological information for Dorset (Eagles 1994; Hase 1994), but although the material is very useful they can hardly be said to have produced any new conclusions. It seems that we are still faced with the fact that Romano-British culture lasted in Dorset into the sixth century and perhaps in parts into the seventh. The very few fifth- and sixth-century Saxon finds can best be explained as belonging to mercenaries and it is not until the seventh century that any number of Saxon burials appear, most of them in and around Dorchester. And it is at Dorchester, or rather Poundbury, that the only evidence for a post-Roman and apparently non-Saxon settlement has been found (Green 1987). Clearly other important discoveries will be made but they will have to be on a massive scale to change my original view that the Saxons came so late to Dorset that it cannot have been they who created the complex arrangements of estates and land units which covered the county by the ninth century.

This linking of land units or estates, and ultimately parishes, so firmly with the Roman period has been, with a few notable exceptions, ignored by most later workers elsewhere, some of whom still see such estates and parishes as being purely Saxon in origin and created either by fusion or fission of earlier estates (Jones 1976; Pythian-Adams 1978; Hooke 1985; Barker and Seaward 1990). Yet the evidence in Dorset is so strong that its implications remain vital to the understanding of Saxon landscapes elsewhere. This is one piece of *Dorset* that, to my regret, has not been taken further.

I used up a great deal of valuable space in *Dorset* describing these land units or tithings, each associated with a settlement and which, grouped together in various combinations, made up the parishes of the county. This over-kill was largely the result of being mesmerized by a phenomenon with which I as a Midlander had never before met. I was used to single-settlement parishes with one field system. To find, for example, that the parish of Charminster had ten tithings and that the eight parishes of south Purbeck had nearly fifty settlements and land units between them, all apparently in existence by the ninth century, was a conceptual shock from which I never recovered.

The original research on which all the evidence for these Dorset estates was based was carried out by a man whom I never met. I have always regretted that he died before I came to work in the county. This was Colonel C D Drew, a truly remarkable man and a great but largely unrecognized landscape historian. His published work was very limited although his article on the manors of the Iwerne valley written as early as 1947 (Drew 1948) was one of the most influential pieces of work I ever read. And his papers in the museum at Dorchester, containing as they did the complete geographical breakdown of Saxon Dorset, were even more important and changed my perception, first of Dorset and then of the whole of the English landscape.

The understanding of these estates or tithings in Dorset also proved immensely valuable when I returned to the Midlands and East Anglia. For the same multiple units of tenure and agriculture actually existed there, although in not quite as complex a form as in Wessex. At first they did not help solve the problem of continuity but they certainly assisted in the understanding of what appeared to be a surplus of medieval settlements in Cambridgeshire and Northamptonshire parishes (Taylor 1972b, 55–9). Later though, and especially in south-west Northamptonshire, I discovered very complex patterns of estates and settlements. There, in and around Kings Sutton parish, I found the nearest parallel to the multiple settlements and tithings of Purbeck but with even better archaeological and historical evidence for their probable Roman and earlier beginnings (Brown and Taylor 1978).

It was in my discussion of continuity in *Dorset* that I examined place-names and explored the possibility that they could be changed through time. This was partly a reaction to having lived at and studied another place which was a major formative influence on me, Whiteparish, Wiltshire (Taylor 1967a). The fact that that village changed its name three times between 1086 and 1190 led me to doubt some of the apparently obvious connections between settlements and their names. In the 1960s I had only Fägersten (1933) on the place names of Dorset with which to work. Now we have the superb volumes by Mills (1977–89) which show only too clearly the dangers of an amateur such as myself dabbling in a very specialized subject. But I remain deeply sceptical about place-names, not with their etymology but with some of the supposed connections between them and the settlements to which they are attached and the conclusions drawn from distributions. This scepticism has been reinforced by an examination that I made of the nineteenth-century place-names in Ontario, Canada. The origins of these names seem to defy many of the accepted conventions but at the same time are firmly and logically based in the social background of the period.

Medieval settlements

From the land units of Dorset I moved on to the settlements within them and especially to what eventually became my principal interest in the English landscape, the problem of the origins and development of medieval rural settlement. In *Dorset* I failed to address the principal issues, and what I wrote now seems muddled, unclear and to avoid the matter of origins almost entirely. On reflection this appears to be curious for, while working in Dorset for the Royal Commission, I came across all types of evidence relating to rural settlement which was later to be put to good use in many articles and lectures. Perhaps *Dorset* was written too early in my career, before my ideas were fully developed but, as R H Worth said, 'one always writes too soon; but if one puts it off, one may not write at all' (Finberg 1967, vii). Nevertheless, considering my later interest in medieval settlements, *Dorset* is strangely empty and reserved. Yet its silence may have been at least partly the result of an unhappiness with the conventional explanations of village origins. For, as I noted earlier, in the late 1960s villages were still assumed to have begun in early Saxon times and to have acquired their shapes by the actions of recently arrived democratic Saxon peasants settling in a strange land. This of course did not apply in Dorset so what could have led to the beginnings of Dorset villages? I did not know then so I dodged the issue. As a result there was nothing at all in *Dorset* about polyfocal villages, although I had seen them and even described them at Combe Keynes and at Whiteparish in Wiltshire (Taylor 1967a; 1967b). Indeed at the time I was writing *Dorset* my extra-mural students in Cambridge had actually coined the term polyfocal and published it (Taylor 1971). Soon after polyfocal villages appeared everywhere (Taylor 1977).

Even worse, there was nothing on what were later to be termed regulated villages and thus no attempt was made to raise the question of planned settlements. Yet again I had seen them on the ground at Chideock and at Puddletown, for example, and on an early map at Winterborne Kingston, but had not understood them. We had to wait for Brian Roberts and other geographers to advance the work of Harry Thorpe in northern England and identify planned villages there (Allerston 1970; Roberts 1973; Shepperd 1976). Even so it was some years before village planning at a late date, in late Saxon or post-Conquest times, was accepted. Now that that has been achieved, we have to solve the more fundamental problem of who planned them – their lords or the peasant community. This remains an unanswered question (Harvey 1989; Dyer 1994a).

My myopia with regard to regulated villages was matched by my failure to recognize the significance of deserted medieval villages. Like the rest of my contemporaries in the late 1960s, deserted villages were of interest to me solely because they had been deserted (Beresford 1954; Barley 1957; Thompson 1960; Biddle 1961–2). The only things that mattered were when, how and why desertion had taken place. I failed to see, as did we all, that it was the shapes of deserted villages rather than the layouts of existing ones that could tell us more about the origins of all villages. I had examined and recorded highly regular deserted Dorset villages such as Holworth, Ringstead and Friarmayne for the Royal Commission (1970a Chaldon Herring [20], Osmington [27], West Knighton [19]). But no connections were made. It has taken me 25 years to correct this error at least with regard to regular Dorset villages, but I have tried to make amends in a recent paper (Taylor 1994). It is, I believe, now possible to see that regulated or planned villages were as common in Dorset as anywhere in England.

What obscures this regular form in most existing villages are the enormous later changes which almost all places in England have undergone. And village change was another omission in *Dorset* which has to be noted and remedied here. Again I failed almost entirely to see what became so obvious later on (Taylor 1979; 1982; Hall 1993). So-called shrunken villages, or SVRs as the Royal Commission called them, dominated my thinking in Dorset. The Royal Commission volumes, for which I wrote most of the medieval settlement sections, are full of shrunken villages – with the emphasis on the shrunken (RCHME 1970a lxvii–lxviii; 1972 xxix). They were all regarded, as their name implies, as the last stage but one in the process of desertion and therefore as less important and interesting than complete desertions. The way they were treated in the Royal Commission volumes, as well as in *Dorset*, shows this.

In fact they are probably more important than the completely deserted settlements in terms of the complex events and situations that led to their reduction in size and more often changes in function and thus in form. Even now shrunken villages are not accepted as important and certainly not by those in charge of the preservation and conservation of our heritage. The remains of more shrunken villages than any other type of archaeological site have been destroyed in the last 25 years all over the country. It is also important to remember that many shrunken villages are not actually shrunken at all but are the result of shifts of settlement in response to all kinds of situations (Taylor 1979; 1983a 151–74). As I now live in an apparently 'shrunken' village, I see perhaps more clearly than most the need for a complete reassessment of this type of settlement remains (Taylor 1989).

Another related aspect of village change not dealt with in *Dorset* was the large-scale alteration of village plans. Perhaps the most remarkable example of a village changing its form entirely is the deserted medieval village of Bardolfstone in Puddletown parish (RCHME 1970b, Puddletown [21]). In *Dorset* I described the site yet still failed to see its significance. It was not until many years later that its importance dawned on me. Once grasped, of course, major changes in village layouts became so obvious that it was hard to understand why they had not been noticed before. In a very short time similar examples came to light first at other deserted villages as at Astwick and later in existing villages as at Culworth, both in Northamptonshire (RCHME 1982, Culworth [2], Evenley [9]). Yet one does not always initially understand what later becomes obvious. Only the other day looking at a Cambridge-shire village which I have seen many times and even described in print, I suddenly realized that its plan was the result of a major change in its original layout.

However, in the end I think I made up for this early lack of understanding of settlement change. This was in the work I carried out for the Royal Commission in Lincolnshire with my old friends and colleagues Paul Everson and Christopher Dunn. There, in a relatively small area, we discovered, recorded, illustrated and discussed almost every conceivable type of village alteration. *Change and Continuity*, the title under which it was finally published, remains one of my most personally satisfying contributions to landscape history (Everson *et al.* 1991).

One final point relating to settlement change and desertion is perhaps worth noting. This was my refusal in *Dorset* to use the, at that time, highly fashionable phrase 'the retreat from the margins'. This term was widely used in the 1960s and 1970s as it seemed to succinctly express all that desertion and shrinkage of settlement implied in the contracting economic and social circumstances of the fourteenth and early fifteenth centuries. In 1970 I was clearly ahead of my time in pointing out that desertion and shrinkage of medieval settlements in

Dorset was in no way connected with the abandonment of marginal land, even though I did not know the actual cause. The problem has been discussed many times since without a great deal of new light being shed until Professor Christopher Dyer, a rare example of a traditional historian who understands landscapes, finally removed the concept of marginal land retreat for good and showed us the way forward (Dyer 1994b).

Fields and farmsteads

There is a great deal in *Dorset* about farmsteads and especially on those in the west and north-west of the county in the former wooded areas which were medieval Royal Forests, as well as on those in the south-eastern heathlands. These farmsteads, together with their irregular-shaped fields which seem to have been cut from the wastes and woods allegedly in the twelfth and thirteenth centuries, fascinated me then and still do. Initially this was because before coming to Wessex I had never seen a landscape created by woodland clearance. I was immediately thrown into one at Whiteparish (Taylor 1967a) and then a few years later sent by the Royal Commission to the Blackmoor Vale (Taylor 1966a). When I came to try to understand the Vale I found what seemed to be the answer in Dorchester Museum. For there, already dog-eared and fading, were bundles of thin carbon copies of the transcripts of the thirteenth-century Forest Eyres and other contemporary documents in the Public Record Office, all mixed up in Colonel Drew's papers. These appeared to be the documented details of the assarting which produced the irregular field patterns as well as of the establishment of many of the associated farmsteads and hamlets. It all seemed to fit into the story of the great economic expansion of the twelfth and thirteenth centuries about which I had learned at university only a few short years before. But even then I had my doubts over the apparently neat correlation between landscape and documents. It was all very well to sit in a lecture theatre being taught the elements of medieval economic growth, or to be cosily tucked away in the library at Dorchester reading long lists of assarts and purprestures. It was quite another thing to stand on the top of the chalk escarpment at Bulbarrow and view what seemed to be the result of a mere 250 years of woodland clearance and associated settlement stretching as far as the eye could see. It all seemed very improbable. And when I saw that Hethfelton Farm on the heathlands of East Stoke is recorded with its two villeins and a slave in Domesday Book and that all the scattered farmsteads now in the ranges in Povington parish north of the Purbeck Ridge also seemed to be there in 1086 (Thorn 1983, 11.8, 30.4, 37.11, 49.14), it was obvious that the accepted story was wrong. As indeed Hoskins had already pointed out was the case in another landscape in Devon (Hoskins 1963).

I began to think that perhaps this process of woodland clearance and heathland reclamation was a much longer one than I had been taught or than the documents implied. So in *Dorset* I daringly suggested that the documents were only recording the very last stage of a process of settlement expansion which had begun in Saxon times. Since then further work all over Britain has indicated that I was probably right, although not perhaps everywhere (Williamson 1986b; 1988; Brown and Taylor 1989; Dyer 1990). But there remain difficulties as to the dating of these dispersed settlements which have not yet been resolved. These problems include a lack of archaeological evidence for the apparent Saxon origins of these farmsteads

(Weddall and Henderson 1992) as well as the fact that the expansion which led to the establishment of some of them is said to have taken place from villages which did not themselves then exist. Further questions arise over the inevitable changes that have taken place at these settlements (Fox 1989).

Of the medieval open fields of Dorset I said little. This was because, as a Midlander who was introduced to massive ridge-and-furrow with all its complications at the age of eight, and who had recorded it in detail in Cambridgeshire (RCHME 1968, lxvi–lxix and *passim*; Taylor 1973, 93–6), I was lost in Dorset for none seemed to exist there. It did of course, especially in north-west Dorset, and I recorded much of it there for the Royal Commission. But it was poor stuff and I could not become interested in it (RCHME 1970b, xlvii; 1972, xxix).

What interested me much more were strip lynchets. I filled a whole page in *Dorset* on them. The reason for this was that again I had never seen them before, although I later found them even in Cambridgeshire (Taylor 1973, 93–6) and only last year, unbelievably, in Norfolk (SMR). One of my earliest tasks for the Royal Commission was to write up the archive for one of the best groups of strip lynchets in Dorset. In those days the width, height and length of every strip had to be measured and recorded and every form of termination noted (RCHME 1970a, Worth Matravers [29]). Since then Worth Matravers has not been my favourite place. There was also a period of high excitement when an article appeared in *Antiquity* claiming that strip lynchets were prehistoric in date (Macnab 1965). I was encouraged by Collin Bowen to write a rejoinder pointing out that strip lynchets had to be medieval (Taylor 1966b). Although I was, of course, basically correct, I have since found cultivation terraces in the north of England that are certainly pre-Roman. I have carefully avoided publishing these.

Much more important than strip lynchets, although hardly dealt with in *Dorset*, were the very slight remains of ridge-and-furrow ploughing overlying earlier prehistoric and Roman fields, which Collin Bowen and Peter Fowler had discovered and analysed in both Dorset and Wiltshire (Bowen 1961 48–50; Bowen and Fowler 1962, 104–6; RCHME 1970a, Ancient Field Groups 1, 15, 23). This type of ploughing was significant because it was a form of cultivation which had not previously been recognized for what it was, that is short-term or temporary cultivation of marginal land probably carried out in the thirteenth or early fourteenth century. O G S Crawford had seen it and published it in the 1920s but had failed to separate it from the underlying prehistoric and Roman field pattern (Crawford 1928, plates XIX, XX, XXII).

Collin Bowen had actually recognized a related form of medieval or later cultivation overlying the extensive prehistoric and Roman field systems at Winterborne Houghton and Turnworth. Yet the accounts in the Royal Commission volume are so circumspect that it is almost impossible to see from them what is clearly there on the ground (RCHME 1970b, Ancient Field Groups 53, 55). In *Dorset* I failed entirely to pick up this. The whole area of these prehistoric fields at Houghton and Turnworth should be re-examined and republished for this later ploughing gives an even greater significance to what are already major national monuments by any standard.

One category of field remains that I included in *Dorset* was that of relict water meadows. These were totally ignored by the Royal Commission, to its everlasting shame. Other scholars have since filled in the gaps in our understanding of these complex and wonderful systems of water management on which so much of the wealth of Dorset agriculture rested from the seventeenth century onwards (Bettey 1977; Bowie 1987). It is also a pleasure to note that my old student Tom Williamson has further enhanced our understanding of this type of agriculture by his discovery of the remains of water meadows in Norfolk and Suffolk (Wade Martins and Williamson 1994).

Parks and gardens

Given my almost total ignorance of architectural history in the 1960s, apart from one or two gaps already noted, my summary of the development and social background of the country houses of Dorset seems in retrospect to have been surprisingly competent. What was lacking though, because the discipline had hardly got beyond the dilettante stage, was an analysis of the settings of these houses in terms of their parks and gardens. On the other hand the long description of the mounts, terraces, ha-has and ponds of the remains of the Bridgeman garden at Eastbury (RCHME 1972, Tarrant Gunville [2]), which went with the short-lived Vanburgh house there, might seem to be the beginnings of a totally new subject, the field archaeology of gardens (Taylor 1983b). In fact this is not so for I first realized in 1960 in Cambridgeshire that relict gardens were not only very common but probably to be found everywhere (RCHME 1968, lxiii, Childerley [4], Gamlingay (61)). Nevertheless on reflection the mention of the Eastbury garden and the smaller one at West Woodyates (RCHME 1975, Pentridge [5]), did represent a step forward in the widening of knowledge and the understanding of the distribution of abandoned gardens. This is another area in which more research in Dorset should produce results. Given that we now know that every county in England has numerous sites of abandoned gardens – for example there are over 40 in Northamptonshire alone (RCHME 1975–85 *passim*) – there must be many more awaiting discovery in Dorset. Some, such as those at Bindon, have already been noted (Keen and Coppeck 1987, 66–8) but there should be others. For example, the earthworks on the south side of Tomson Farm, at Winterborne Tomson, described by the Royal Commission as medieval settlement remains (RCHME 1970b, Anderson [6]), are actually the site of a formal garden probably of early seventeenth-century date and perhaps created when the house was rebuilt.

But although I was at the forefront of garden archaeology in 1970 I ignored the much more important existing gardens. There is no mention in *Dorset* of the nineteenth-century gardens at Abbotsbury, now a Grade I site on the English Heritage Register of Parks and Gardens. Nor is there any reference to those at Cranborne Manor or Forde Abbey. And there is only a brief reference to that most wonderful of all Dorset gardens, at Athelhampton, laid out by Inigo Thomas in the 1890s and now also a Grade I site (English Heritage 1987).

Parks too received short shrift in *Dorset*. The great ones at Milton Abbas, Wimborne St Giles, Sherborne, Charborough and Melbury Sampford were all noted, as were the estate villages at Milton and Crichel. But the landscapes of the parks were not discussed and the mid nineteenth-century village of Bridehead at Little Bredy was forgotten (Pevsner and Newman 1972, 254). A new *Dorset* would need a whole section on designed landscapes to catch up with advances in scholarship.

Towns

There were some dreadful errors and omissions in *Dorset* where towns were concerned. I failed to see the outlines of the Saxon burgh in the plan of Bridport and merely followed the already discredited identification of Bredie as the Old Warren hillfort (Symonds 1922). I missed the fact that both Cranborne and Cerne Abbas, for example, were probably baronial and monastic plantations respectively and that Corfe Castle is perhaps also a planted town.

The problem was that inevitably I was writing within the confines of knowledge of the late 1960s. At that time Maurice Beresford had just published *New Towns of the Middle Ages* (1967) which changed the way we all looked at urban beginnings and which was an enormous influence on me. As a result in *Dorset* I correctly noted the planned twelfth-century origins of Poole, Melcombe and Weymouth as well as of the lost Newton on the south side of Poole Harbour (Bowen and Taylor 1964). I also equally correctly pointed to the late Saxon planned beginnings of Wareham, Shaftesbury, Wimborne (Taylor 1968) and, within its earlier walls, Dorchester. But Beresford's definition of a town was extraordinarily limiting. Later workers, both nationally and locally, have improved our understanding of the growth and origins of towns enormously and anything that I said in *Dorset* has long been overtaken by new information and ideas (Platt 1976; Aston and Bond 1976; Hodges 1982; Keen 1984). I think that there is now considerable scope for a re-examination of very small towns in both Dorset and elsewhere, especially in relation to their probably quite late origins. The plan-form of many of them seems to me to suggest an element of conscious creation or improvement even if documentary proof is lacking. The 'planned' elements may be minimal and may have been created after the initial development as urban centres, but they must imply some deliberate alteration, addition or extension to an existing place, specifically for marketing purposes. This being so, I would suggest that Blandford, Sturminster Newton, Beaminster, Milton Abbas and Bere Regis are among places worthy of examination in terms of their commercial beginnings (Pern 1980).

Of the more recent history of the towns of the county I wrote very little in *Dorset*. There would have been much better accounts of the larger urban areas such as Weymouth and Poole if I had had the works of a later generation of urban and architectural historians who have shown us both how modern towns grew and why they look like they do (Dyos 1961; Oliver *et al.* 1981; Muthesius 1982).

There were a number of other aspects of the landscape of the county which were dealt with inadequately in *Dorset*. The study of vernacular buildings, which has been greatly advanced locally by the work of Bob Machin (1978), is an example, although I am conscious that the subject, at least in terms of landscape, seems to be running out of steam and there is little new to say at the moment.

The Church, both its physical presence and the results of its political and economic control, is also a subject which would repay further investigation. Again the study of ecclesiastical buildings in Dorset has not greatly advanced in the last 20 years. Has it been stifled by the magisterial and apparently complete Royal Commission survey? There have been a number of new and exciting ideas concerning churches but few of these have been applied to Dorset (Richmond, 1986; Morris, 1989). The study of the impact of the early Church with its minsters and *pariochae* has certainly progressed as can be seen by the recent paper by

Patrick Hase (1994). But there is still plenty of scope for an examination of the effect of the Church and especially that of the monastic houses on the land they owned. The planning of and alterations to villages spring to mind as well as changes to rivers and other watercourses. The way forward has been indicated by Aston (1993, chapter 7), but his suggestions have yet to be fully taken up.

One last and complete omission in *Dorset* must be noted, that of what might be termed 'historical ecology'. In 1970 this subject had not been invented so perhaps a mere historian may be forgiven for not thinking of it. But the debt all landscape historians now owe to that small band of ecologists, most notably Oliver Rackham, who have developed this subject is immense. They have transformed the way we look at the landscape as much as anyone in the last 25 years and *Dorset* as it stands is the poorer for having been written before their ideas gained common currency (Rackham 1976; 1986).

In this paper I have tried to put *Dorset* into its correct place within the history of landscape studies. That is, as merely one building block out of many that have gone to help us understand the making of the English landscape. There have been many more blocks laid since 1970. But I fear that we have still only reached foundation level.

Bibliography

In a paper of this nature and length it would be impossible to cite every book and paper that is or has been relevant to landscape studies in Dorset and beyond. I have therefore tried to list only those works, apart from my own, which in various ways have influenced me the most over some 40 years.

Addison, P, 1989, Excavation of Neolithic and Bronze Age pits, and a section of Roman road on a pipeline near Lodge Farm, Pamphill, Dorset. *Proceedings of the Dorset Natural History and Archaeological Society*, 111, 15–29

Allerston, P, 1970, English village development. *Transactions of the Institute of British Geographers*, 51, 95–109

Allcroft, A H, 1908, *Earthwork of England*. London. Macmillan and Co

Arnold, C J, 1984, *Roman Britain to Saxon England*. London. Croom Helm

Ashworth, C, 1986, *Military Airfields in Central South and South-East*. Wellingborough. Patrick Stephens

Aston, M, 1989, The development of rural settlement in Somerset. In R Higham (ed), *Landscape and Townscape in the South-West* (= Exeter Studies in History 22). Exeter. Exeter University Press. 19–40

Aston, M, 1993, *Monasteries*. London. Batsford

Aston, M, and Bond, J, 1976, *The Landscape of Towns*. London. Dent

Balchin, W G V, 1955, *Cornwall*. London. Hodder and Stoughton

Barker, K, and Seaward, D R, 1990, Boundaries and landscape in Blackmoor. *Proceedings of the Dorset Natural History and Archaeological Society*, 112, 5–22

Barley, M W, 1957, Cistercian land clearances in Nottinghamshire. *Nottingham Medieval Studies*, 1, 75–89

Barratt, J, Bradley, R, and Green, M, 1991, *Landscape, Monuments and Society: The Prehistory of Cranborne Chase*. Cambridge. Cambridge University Press

Barratt, J, Bradley, R, and Hall, M, (eds), 1991, *Papers on the Prehistoric Archaeology of Cranborne Chase* (= Oxbow Monograph 11). Oxford. Oxbow Books

Beresford, M W, 1954, *The Lost Villages of England*. London. Lutterworth

Beresford, M W, 1957, *History on the Ground*. London. Lutterworth

Beresford, M W, 1967, *New Towns of the Middle Ages*. London. Lutterworth

Beresford, M W, and St Joseph, J K S, 1958, *Medieval England: An Aerial Survey*. Cambridge. Cambridge University Press

Bettey, J H, 1977, The development of water meadows in Dorset. *Agricultural History Review*, 25, 37–43

Biddle, M, 1961–2, The deserted medieval village of Seacourt, Berkshire. *Oxoniensia*, 26–7, 70–201

Bonney, D J, 1966, Pagan Saxon burials and boundaries in Wiltshire. *Wiltshire Archaeological Magazine*, 61, 25–30

Bonney, D J, 1976, Early boundaries and estates in southern England. In P Sawyer (ed), *Medieval Settlement: Continuity and Change*. London. Edward Arnold. 72–82

Bowen, H C, 1961, *Ancient Fields*. London. British Association for the Advancement of Science

Bowen, H C, and Fowler, P J, 1962, The archaeology of Fyfield and Overton Downs. *Wiltshire Archaeological Magazine*, 58, 98–115

Bowen, H C, and Taylor, C C, 1964, The site of Newton, Dorset. *Medieval Archaeology*, 8, 223–6

Bowie, G S, 1987, Water meadows in Wessex. *Agricultural History Review*, 35, 151–8

Bradley, R, 1978, *The Prehistoric Settlement of Britain*. London. Routledge

Bradley R, and Edmonds, M, 1993, *Interpreting the Axe Trade*. Cambridge. Cambridge University Press

Brown, A E, and Taylor, C C, 1989, The origins of dispersed settlement. *Landscape History*, 11, 61–81

Brown, A E, and Taylor, C C, 1991, *Moated Sites in North Bedfordshire* (= University of Leicester Vaughan Papers 35). Leicester. University of Leicester

Brown, F, and Taylor, C C, 1978, Settlement and land use in Northamptonshire. In B Cunliffe and T Rowley (eds), *Lowland Iron Age Communities in Europe* (= BAR International Series 48). Oxford. British Archaeological Reports. 77–89

Crawford, O G S, 1953, *Archaeology in the Field*. London. Phoenix House

Crawford, O G S, and Keiller, A, 1928, *Wessex from the Air*. Oxford. Oxford University Press

Collingwood, R G, and Myers, J N L, 1936, *Roman Britain and the English Settlements*. Oxford. Clarendon Press

Cox, P W, and Hearne, C M, 1991, *Reclaimed from the Heath* (= DNHAS Monograph 9). Dorchester. Dorset Natural History and Archaeological Society

Darby, H C, 1936, *The Medieval Fenland*. Cambridge. Cambridge University Press

Darby, H C, 1940, *The Draining of the Fens*. Cambridge. Cambridge University Press

Drew, C D, 1948, The manors of the Iwerne Valley. *Proceedings of the Dorset Natural History and Archaeological Society*, 69, 45–8

Drury, P, and Rodwell, W, 1980, Settlement in the later Iron Age and Roman periods. In D G Buckley (ed), *The Archaeology of Essex to AD 1500* (= CBA Research Report 34). London. Council for British Archaeology. 59–75

Dyer, C, 1990, Dispersed settlement in medieval England. *Medieval Archaeology*, 34, 97–121

Dyer, C, 1994a, Power and conflict in the medieval English village. In C Dyer, *Everyday Life in Medieval England*. London. Hambledon. 1–12

Dyer, C, 1994b, The retreat from marginal land. In C Dyer, *Everyday Life in Medieval England.* London. Hambledon. 13–26

Dyos, H J, 1961, *Victorian Suburb.* Leicester. Leicester University Press

Eagles, B, 1994, The archaeological evidence for settlement in the fifth to seventh centuries AD. In M Aston and C Lewis (eds), *The Medieval Landscape of Wessex* (= Oxbow Monograph 46). Oxford. Oxbow Books. 13–32

English Heritage, 1987, *Register of Parks and Gardens: Part 12 Dorset.* London. English Heritage

Everitt, A, 1986, *Continuity and Colonisation: The Evolution of Kentish Settlement.* Leicester. Leicester University Press

Everson, P L, Taylor, C C, and Dunn, C J, 1991, *Change and Continuity: Rural Settlement in North-West Lincolnshire.* London. HMSO

Fägersten, A, 1933, *The Place-Names of Dorset.* Uppsala. A-B Lundequistska Bokhandeln

Finberg, H P R, 1955, *Gloucestershire.* London. Hodder and Stoughton

Finberg, H P R, (ed), 1967, *The Agrarian History of England and Wales. Volume 4.* Cambridge. Cambridge University Press

Fleming, A, 1988, *The Dartmoor Reaves.* London. Batsford

Ford, W J, 1976, Settlement patterns in the central region of the Warwickshire Avon. In P Sawyer (ed), *Medieval Settlement: Continuity and Change.* London. Edward Arnold. 274–94

Fowler, P J, 1983, *The Farming of Prehistoric Britain.* Cambridge. Cambridge University Press

Fox, C, 1952, *The Personality of Britain* (4th edition). Cardiff. National Museum of Wales

Fox, H S A, 1989, Peasant farmers, patterns of settlement and pays in landscape and townscape in the south-west. In R Higham (ed), *Landscape and Townscape in the South West* (= Exeter Studies in History 22). Exeter. University of Exeter Press. 41–73

Frere, S, 1987, *Britannia* (3rd edition). London. Routledge

Fulford, M, 1990, The landscape of Roman Britain. *Landscape Historian*, 12, 25–32

Green, C S, 1987, *Excavations at Poundbury I* (= DNHAS Monograph 7). Dorchester. Dorset Natural History and Archaeological Society

Gunther, R T, 1928, *The Architecture of Roger Pratt.* London. Oxford. Oxford University Press

Hall, D, and Coles, J, 1994, *Fenland Survey: An Essay in Landscape and Persistence* (= English Heritage Archaeological Report 1). London. English Heritage

Hall, T, 1993, Witchampton: Village origins. *Proceedings of the Dorset Natural History and Archaeological Society*, 115, 121–32

Harvey, P D A, 1989, Initiative and authority in settlement change. In M Aston, D Austin and C Dyer (eds), *The Rural Settlements of Medieval England.* Oxford. Blackwell. 31–44

Hase, P H, 1994, The church in the Wessex heartland. In M Aston and C Lewis (eds), *The Medieval Landscape of Wessex* (= Oxbow Monograph 46). Oxford. Oxbow Books. 47–82

Hawkes, C F C, 1959, The ABC of the British Iron Age. *Antiquity*, 33, 170–82

Hodges, R, 1982, *Dark Age Economics: The Origins of Towns and Trade AD 600–1000.* London. Duckworth

Hooke, D, 1982, The Anglo-Saxon landscape. In T R Slater and P J Jarvis (eds), *Field and Forest: An Historical Geography of Warwickshire and Worcestershire.* Norwich. Geo Books. 79–103

Hooke, D, 1985, *The Kingdom of the Hwicce.* Manchester. Manchester University Press

Hoskins, W G, 1955, *The Making of the English Landscape.* London. Hodder and Stoughton

Hoskins, W G, 1957, *Leicestershire.* London. Hodder and Stoughton

Hoskins, W G, 1963, The Highland Zone in Domesday Book. In *Provincial England.* London. Macmillan. 15–52

Jones, G R J, 1976, Multiple estates and early settlement. In P Sawyer (ed), *Medieval Settlement: Continuity and Change*. London. Edward Arnold. 15–40

Keen, L, 1984, The towns of Dorset. In J Haslem (ed), *Anglo-Saxon Towns in Southern England*. Chichester. Phillimore. 203–47

Keen, L, and Coppeck, A, 1978, *Historic Landscapes of the Weld Estate*. Dorset. The Weld Estate.

Lucas, R N, 1993, *The Romano-British Villa at Halstock* (= DNHAS Monograph 13). Dorchester. Dorset Natural History and Archaeological Society

Machin, R, 1978, *The Houses of Yetminster*. Bristol. University of Bristol, Department of Extra-Mural Studies

Macnab, J W, 1965, British strip lynchets. *Antiquity*, 39, 279– 90

Maitland, F W, 1897, *Domesday Book and Beyond*. Cambridge. Cambridge University Press

Mercer, R, (ed), 1981, *Farming Practice in British Prehistory*. Edinburgh. Edinburgh University Press

Mills, A D, 1977–89, *The Place-Names of Dorset* (English Place-Name Society Volumes LII, LIII and LIX/LX). London. The English Place-Names Society. (3 vols)

Milward, R, 1955, *Lancashire*. London. Hodder and Stoughton

Moore, W F, and Ross, M S, 1989, The Romano-British settlement at Gillingham. *Proceedings of the Dorset Natural History and Archaeological Society*, 111, 57–70

Morris, R, 1989, *Churches in the Landscape*. London. Dent

Muthesius, S, 1982, *The English Terraced House*. London. Yale University Press

Norfolk SMR, 1993, *Norfolk County Sites and Monuments Record: Cockthorpe Parish Report*. Gressenhall. Norfolk County Council. [SMR typescript report]

Oliver, P, Davis, I, and Bentley, J, 1981, *Dunroamin: The Suburban Semi and its Enemies*. London. Barrie and Jenkins

Pern, K J, 1980, *Historic Towns in Dorset* (= DNHAS Monograph 1). Dorchester. Dorset Natural History and Archaeological Society

Pevsner, N, and Newman, J, 1972, *Dorset*. London. Penguin

Piggott, S, 1954, *Neolithic Cultures of the British Isles*. Cambridge. Cambridge University Press

Platt, C, 1976, *The English Medieval Town*. London. Martin Secker and Warburg

Pythian-Adams, C, 1978, *Continuity, Fields and Fission* (Leicester University, Department of English Local History Occasional Paper (3rd Series) 4). Leicester. Leicester University Press

Rackham, O, 1976, *Trees and Woodland in the British Landscape*. London. Dent

Rackham, O, 1986, *The History of the Countryside*. London. Dent

Richmond, H, 1986, Outlines of church development in Northamptonshire. In L A S Butler and R K Morris (eds), *The Anglo-Saxon Church* (= CBA Research Report 60). London. Council for British Archaeology. 176–87

Richmond, I A, 1955, *Roman Britain*. Harmondsworth. Penguin

Riley, D N, 1980, *Early Landscapes from the Air*. Sheffield. Department of Prehistory and Archaeology, University of Sheffield

Roberts, B K, 1973, Village plans in County Durham. *Medieval Archaeology*, 21, 33–55

Rodwell, W, 1978, Relict landscapes in Essex. In C Bowen and P Fowler (eds) *Early Land Allotment* (= BAR British Series 48). Oxford. British Archaeological Reports. 89–98

Ross, M S, 1987, Kington Magna: A fieldwalking survey of the prehistory. *Proceedings of the Dorset Natural History and Archaeological Society*, 109, 91–104

RCHME, 1968, *An Inventory of Historical Monuments in the County of Cambridge. Volume One. West Cambridgeshire*. London. HMSO

RCHME, 1970a, *An Inventory of Historical Monuments in the County of Dorset. Volume Two. South-East Dorset*. London. HMSO. (3 parts)

RCHME, 1970b, *An Inventory of Historical Monuments in the County of Dorset. Volume Three. Central Dorset*. London. HMSO. (2 parts)

RCHME, 1972, *An Inventory of Historical Monuments in the County of Dorset. Volume Four. North Dorset*. London. HMSO

RCHME, 1975a, *An Inventory of Historical Monuments in the County of Dorset. Volume Five. East Dorset*. London. HMSO

RCHME, 1975b, *An Inventory of the Historical Monuments in the County of Northampton. Volume I. Archaeological Sites in North-East Northamptonshire*. London. HMSO

RCHME, 1979, *An Inventory of the Historical Monuments in the County of Northampton. Volume II. Archaeological Sites in Central Northamptonshire*. London. HMSO

RCHME, 1981, *An Inventory of the Historical Monuments in the County of Northampton. Volume III. Archaeological Sites in North-West Northamptonshire*. London. HMSO

RCHME, 1982, *An Inventory of the Historical Monuments in the County of Northampton. Volume IV. Archaeological Sites in South-West Northamptonshire*. London. HMSO

Salway, P H, 1981, *Roman Britain*. Oxford. Clarendon Press

Sharples, N M, 1991, *Maiden Castle. Excavations and Field Survey 1985–6* (= Historic Buildings and Monuments Commission for England Archaeological Report 19). London. English Heritage

Shepperd, J A, 1976, Medieval village planning in Northern England. *Journal of Historical Geography*, 2, 3–20

Sunter, N, and Woodward, P J, 1987, *Romano-British Industries in Purbeck* (= DNHAS Monograph 6). Dorchester. Dorset Natural History and Archaeological Society

Symons, M, 1922, Bridport as an Anglo-Saxon mint. *Numismatic Chronicle* (series 5), 2, 144–5

Taylor, C C, 1966a, The pattern of medieval settlement in the Forest of Blackmoor. *Proceedings of the Dorset Natural History and Archaeological Society*, 87, 251–4

Taylor, C C, 1966b, Strip lynchets. *Antiquity*, 40, 277–84

Taylor, C C, 1967a, Whiteparish. *Wiltshire Archaeological Magazine*, 62, 79–101

Taylor, C C, 1967b, Lost Dorset place-names. *Proceedings of the Dorset Natural History and Archaeological Society*, 88, 207–15

Taylor, C C, 1967c, Late Roman pastoral farming in Wessex. *Antiquity*, 41, 304–6

Taylor, C C, 1968, Wimborne Minster. *Proceedings of the Dorset Natural History and Archaeological Society*, 89, 168–9

Taylor, C C, 1970, *Dorset*. London. Hodder and Stoughton

Taylor, C C, 1972a, Settlement patterns in pre-Saxon England. In P Ucko, R Tringham and G W Dimbleby (eds), *Man, Settlement and Urbanism*. London. Duckworth. 109–13

Taylor, C C, 1972b, Maps, documents and fieldwork. In E Fowler (ed) *Field Survey in British Archaeology*. London. Council for British Archaeology. 55–9

Taylor, C C, 1973, *The Cambridgeshire Landscape*. London. Hodder and Stoughton

Taylor, C C, 1975, Roman settlements in the Nene Valley. In P Fowler (ed), *Recent Work in Rural Archaeology*. Bradford-upon Avon. Moonraker Press. 107–19

Taylor, C C, 1977, Polyfocal settlement and the English village. *Medieval Archaeology*, 21, 189–93

Taylor, C C, 1979, Aspects of village mobility in medieval and later times. In S Limbrey and J G Evans (eds), *The Effect of Man on the Landscape: The Lowland Zone* (= CBA Research Report 21). London. Council for British Archaeology. 126–34

Taylor, C C, 1982, Medieval market grants and village morphology. *Landscape History*, 4, 21–8

Taylor, C C, 1983a, *Village and Farmstead*. London. George Phillip

Taylor, C C, 1983b, *The Archaeology of Gardens*. Aylesbury. Shire

Taylor, C C, 1989, Whittlesford: The study of a river-edge village. In M Aston, D Austin and C Dyer (eds), *The Rural Settlements of Medieval England*. Oxford. Blackwell. 207–27

Taylor, C C, 1994, The regular village plan: Dorset revisited and revised. In M Aston and C Lewis (eds), *The Medieval Landscape of Wessex* (= Oxbow Monograph 46). Oxford. Oxbow Books. 213–18

Taylor, C C, (ed), 1971, *Domesday to Dormitory*. Cambridge. WEA

Thompson, F H, 1960, The deserted medieval village of Riseholme, Lincoln. *Medieval Archaeology*, 4, 95–108

Thorn, C and F, 1983, *Domesday Book. 7 Dorset*. Chichester. Phillimore

Thorpe, H, 1951, The green villages of Durham. *Transactions of the Institute of British Geographers*, 15, 49–58

Wade Martins, S, and Williamson, T, 1994, Floated water·meadows in Norfolk. *Agricultural History Review*, 42, 20–37

Wainwright, G J, 1979, *Gussage All Saints: An Iron Age Settlement in Dorset* (= DoE Archaeological Report 10). London. HMSO

Weddell, P, and Henderson, C, 1992, Roadford and Saunton Down in context. *Medieval Settlement Research Group Annual Report*, 7, 6

Whiffen, M, 1950, *Thomas Archer*. London. Batsford

Whimster, R, 1989, *The Emerging Past*. London. Royal Commission on the Historical Monuments of England

Williamson, T, 1984, The Roman countryside: Settlement and agriculture in north-west Essex. *Britannia*, 15, 225–30

Williamson, T, 1986a, Parish boundaries and early fields. *Journal of Historical Geography*, 12, 241–8

Williamson, T, 1986b, The development of settlement in north-west Essex. *Essex Archaeology and History*, 17, 120–32

Williamson, T, 1988, Explaining regional landscapes. *Landscape History*, 10, 5–13

Woodward, P J, 1991, *The South Dorset Ridgeway* (= DNHAS Monograph 8). Dorchester. Dorset Natural History and Archaeological Society

3 *Lamberde leie, dillameres dic*: A lost or a living landscape?

Della Hooke

Introduction

The study of place-names has always been an exact discipline, requiring knowledge and experience, but the relationship of place-names to settlement and landscape studies has often been something of a free-for-all with, at times, some very strange conclusions being drawn. But perhaps this is as it should be: it should be possible to throw out new ideas and test hypotheses if advances in understanding are to be made – providing there is an attempt to submit these to rigorous academic appraisal.

Place-name chronology and settlement

Perhaps the most obvious change over the last few decades has been the loss of confidence in place-names being able to tell us very much about the date and nature of the settlements themselves. As late as 1977, Domesday Book entries were being seen unequivocally as 'villages', suggesting the individual nucleated settlements that term implies (Darby 1977). But Domesday Book gives us the name of manors, not single settlements, and a name might, of course, cover a dozen dispersed farms as easily as a single nucleation. Few would now dispute this but there is still a tendency to regard names as positive indicators of static settlements.

First, it should be made clear that we rarely have any notion of the name by which early Anglo-Saxon settlements were known; we are as ignorant of these as of their Romano-British predecessors. How useful it might be if we could know whether the scattered farms which seem to have been the most characteristic feature of this period bore British or Germanic names or a combination of the two, but this is something that is lost for ever. At a recent conference[1] a question was raised about Mucking, the well-known Anglo-Saxon settlement and cemetery complex beside the Thames in Essex. While settlement at Mucking dates from the first half of the sixth century there were several separate phases of building in successive periods as the settlement shifted across the site. Which, if any, of these referred to the Anglo-Saxon *Mucinga*, 'Muca's people', a name not recorded until it found its way into Domesday Book? Although Gordon Copley in 1986 analyzed the place-names that occur in close proximity to archaeological sites of the fifth and sixth centuries he was well aware that

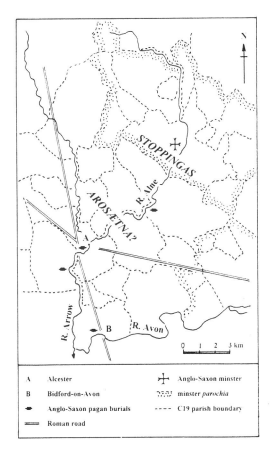

Fig. 3.1. The territory of the Stoppingas, *Warwickshire.*

A	Alcester	╬	Anglo-Saxon minster
B	Bidford-on-Avon		minster *parochia*
●	Anglo-Saxon pagan burials	----	C19 parish boundary
══	Roman road		

'whatever the place-name now associated with an early site, there must be great uncertainty in most instances whether it is the original name'. (Copley 1986, 1).

I would go much further than this and argue that the present settlement name is probably only rarely that of the earliest Anglo-Saxon settlement. Some of the earliest names, indeed, are regional or locational names rather than settlement names and are direct translations of earlier British ones. As an example, the great outlier of oolitic limestone which dominates the Worcestershire Plain as a herald of the Cotswold escarpment bears the British term *bre*, a hill, compounded with Old English *dun*, a hill, and has today further acquired the suffix 'hill', probably because successive generations forgot the actual meaning was already present in the place-name and added the term currently in most common usage. In this case, the name did become attached to a settlement but one which probably only originated at a later date. The fact that the term *tun* was the one Copley found to be 'the one most frequently associated with sites of the pagan period' (1986, 5) shows how false the correlation of archaeological site and place-name may be, for this term seems only rarely to have been in use before the mid eighth century (Cox 1975–6).

Sadly, confidence in a chronology of place-names has steadily been eroded and Copley was forced to admit that 'all in all, the tentative conclusions reached' in his study were 'disappointingly negative. Several hypotheses propounded during the last decade or so have been found to be dependent upon unsatisfactory evidence which was, in any case, selective evidence' (Copley 1986, 20). This does not mean that we have to discard all previous work. John Dodgson's work on the *-ingas, -inga-* place-names in 1966, amplified in the case of Sussex by Martin Welch in 1983, had already shown that locationally these were secondary to the early phase of Anglo-Saxon pagan burial and are probably more closely related to a later period of Anglo-Saxon consolidation and expansion. There is a neat example of an *ingas* type territory in Warwickshire where the *Stoppingas*, recorded in an eighth-century charter (Sawyer 1968, S 94; Birch 1885–99, B 157), were apparently holding a block of land across the headwaters of the River Alne on the margins of the Arden woodland (Figure 3.1), when a minster was established in their territory between AD 716 and AD 737. This area, too, was secondary to pagan burials located in the Arrow and Alne valley and to the earlier Roman town of Alcester. If the territory of the *Stoppingas* (wrongly located by Copley) is to be equated with the medieval *parochia* of this minster then it was assessed at just short of 50 hides (Hooke 1985a, 136; Hooke forthcoming a). Neither is any doubt cast upon the value of Cox's work in identifying those place-name terms most commonly found in early documents. Subsequent work by Gelling (1978) and other scholars has shown how frequently focal estates bore names of a topographical type, a form of name-giving earlier common among the Romans. What indeed, could be more natural than to refer to a prominent local landmark in the vicinity? This has probably been the commonest form of name-giving throughout the world.

Before moving on, I might mention one of the most recent ventures into this investigation of place-names and early archaeology or history. In a recent volume of *Landscape History*, Christopher Balkwill examined the relationship of *wic*, and more especially *wicham*, names to territorial divisions (Balkwill 1993). He attempted to show that such names had originated in administrative divisions older than the hundred, in districts which were 'the basis of early English settlement' (Balkwill 1993, 11). Readers may draw their own conclusions about this but Balkwill's article shows that the debate is still alive and well. It is important to bear in mind the fact that names can and do change. There is a Worcestershire charter for an estate on Bredon Hill (Sawyer 1968, S 1363; Robertson 1939, no 64) that refers to the place known in AD 990 as *Mortune* (Moreton) but which was also named by another name *Uppthrop* (Upthorp) (Hooke 1990, 153). Similarly, the Worcestershire charters record a settlement on the boundary of Bengeworth which was alternatively named *Poticot* or *Potintun*, even erroneously *Potingdun* (Hooke 1985b, 135–7), but this obviously conveyed some confusion as to whether the settlement should be judged representative of a *cot* or a *tun*.

There are even dangers in correlating place-names with later settlements. Obviously most names referred to settlement of some kind but Christopher Taylor (1983) has shown how careful one needs to be in this field. While names may change, as noted above, some place-name scholars seem to forget that settlements themselves have been subject to enormous changes over the thousand or so years that have elapsed since these names were first recorded. Indeed, one may be on safer ground with the little farmsteads referred to in charter boundaries, most of which, like *Poticot,* have subsequently disappeared, than in assuming that a present-day settlement is necessarily still on its Anglo-Saxon site. Furthermore, if a settlement was taking its name from an obvious well-marked natural feature in the immediate locality the settlement itself need not necessarily be exactly on or beside that feature. In the case of settlements bearing a name containing Old English *eg* there is a stronger argument: if places such as Ely were located upon islands of slightly higher ground in the Fens then they are likely to have remained in such a location; Chimney in Oxfordshire is another example where the modern settlement occupies a gravel rise above the floodplain of the Thames. But in the case of hill names, for instance, a settlement bearing the name of the hill could be located almost anywhere in its vicinity: in Worcestershire, Bredon village lies some 3 km from the foot of Bredon Hill, on land only just rising above the floodplain of the River Avon, and other settlements around the foot of the hill bear quite different names (Figure 3.2). Here it does look as if Bredon was a 'primary' settlement in that it became the

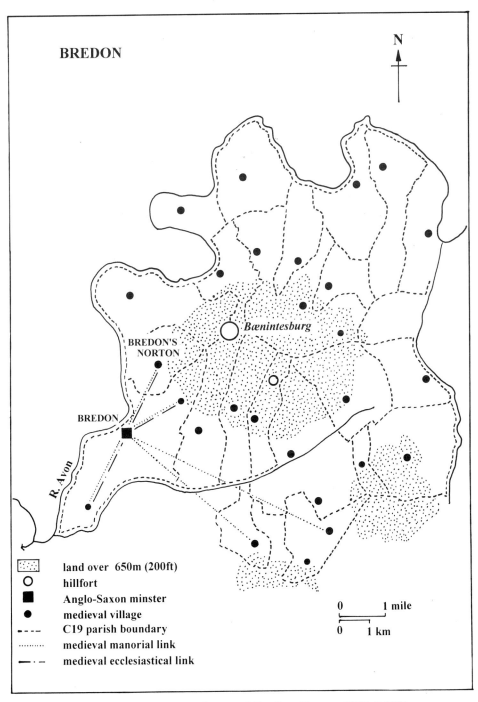

BREDON

N

BREDON'S
NORTON

Bænintesburg

BREDON

R. Avon

land over 650m (200ft)
hillfort
Anglo-Saxon minster
medieval village
C19 parish boundary
medieval manorial link
medieval ecclesiastical link

0   1 mile
0   1 km

Fig. 3.2. Pre-Conquest charter of Crediton (Sawyer 1968, S 255).

site of an early Anglo-Saxon minster while Bredon's Norton on the west flank of the hill was obviously secondary to the main estate, in hierarchy if not in date, although the *tun* name suggests the latter, and many of the other settlements around the hill also bear *tun* names which are likely to be of relatively late origin.

There is one very good argument for the coining of new place-names in the later Anglo-Saxon period: this is that it was at this date that settlement patterns were beginning to undergo massive change. Administrative units until the middle of the Anglo-Saxon period seem to have been relatively large. This does not necessarily mean that they were ancient or British, but that territorial organization was more often based upon the region or the multiple estate than any smaller land unit. This reflects a change in society and land holding which had long-term economic repercussions. John Blair recently summarized this effectively in his book on *Anglo-Saxon Oxfordshire* when he interpreted the emergence of the *tun* settlements, in particular, as evidence 'of the shift from a food-render regime to organized production on demesne farms' (Blair 1994, 79). Large estates were becoming increasingly fragmented in the middle and later Anglo-Saxon periods as portions were leased out to individuals as sub-tenancies. Almost all major ecclesiastical houses leased out small estates, or proto-manors, in this way. As manorial lords also began to establish churches of their own upon these estates so the basis was laid for the ecclesiastical parish which tended to split off from the jurisdiction of the mother church, although part of the once large minster *parochia*.

An example of late Anglo-Saxon estate structure is found in the parish of Tredington, in Worcestershire at the time of Domesday Book but now in Warwickshire (Figure 3.3): the estates of Longdon, Blackwell, Darlingscott etc, were leased out at intervals from within the main estate but Tredington was a minster church which did not permit these to become independent parishes, retaining control of its home estates in one large ecclesiastical parish. Further to the south, Shipston and Tidmingdon, also held, like Tredington, by the Church of Worcester, were, however, allowed to become separate parishes. The *tun* element seems to come into frequent usage only as these sub-manors were coming into existence. One imagines that the new manorial lord might have established his residence in the heart of his manor or in some suitable location which may or may not have already been a settlement site and, if circumstances were right, this would eventually attract more settlement, especially if a church was established there, eventually leading to more or less complete nucleation, a form of settlement I envisage best fitted the Old English term *tun*. In western England *tun* was not confined to small village communities for, if Costen (1992) is correct, it was being used for major estate centres in Somerset. I wonder if this reflects the late emergence of Anglo-Saxon patterns in this region where new Anglo-Saxon centres were replacing their earlier British counterparts so much later than in eastern and midland England.

Nucleation, however, did not occur everywhere. I risk trespassing upon the fields of other contributors but it is necessary to differentiate those regions of intensive cultivation where nucleation tended to occur in conjunction with the development of open field farming from those regions where dispersed settlements continued to support a more pastoral economy. These regions are represented by very different name forms.

It should also be recognized that many settlements came into being as the result of medieval colonization and that their names are not always easy to distinguish from earlier forms. Of

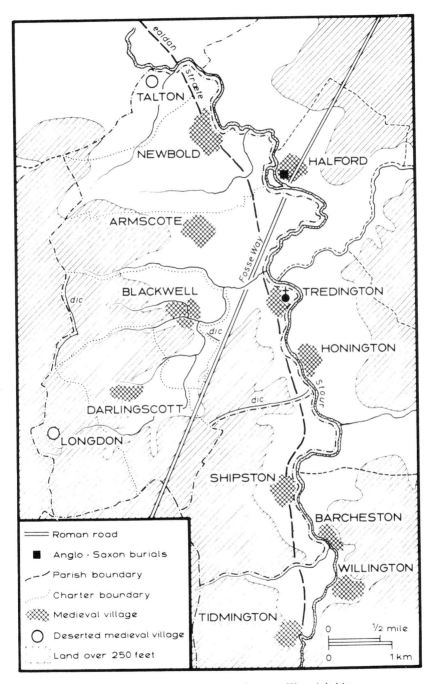

Fig. 3.3. Estate patterns in Tredington, Warwickshire.

31

course the date at which a settlement is first recorded is no indication of its date of origin but there has often been a tendency to push the foundation dates of modern settlements back as early as possible. In a paper published in 1992, Costen argued that the *wyrth* settlements of Somerset 'are representatives of a system of agriculture which preceded the open-field system', implying an origin in a pre-Conquest context, basing his arguments upon Smith's (1956, 273–4) suggestion that the word had ceased to have an active life by the post-Norman period and the fact that by the later historical period so many were lost sites known only from field-names. This argument is, however, refuted for Devon by Svensson (1992) who notes the concentration of the related *-worthig* element on the heaths and moorlands of the north-western corner of that county and shows that he has been able to identify some of the actual colonists who established them. He argues, for instance, that Gulworthy in Tavistock took its name from a certain Roger *Golle* who lived in Tavistock in 1333 and concludes that the 'very high percentage (72%) of personal adjuncts of these names suggests that they represent land brought into cultivation and worked by single individuals' and that many 'were named after the enterprising countrymen who first established them' (Svensson 1992, 59). In apparent confirmation of this, it is interesting to note how neither of the *worth* settlements excavated at Roadford have produced any evidence pre-dating the twelfth century.

But if place-names tell us little that is reliable about dating, there is little doubt that, whatever their shortcomings as a tool of historical analysis, they do tell us a great deal about the nature of the Anglo-Saxon landscape.

Place-names and landscape

Few have contributed more to the debate about the exact interpretation of place-name elements than Dr Margaret Gelling. Her book *Place-names in the Landscape* published in 1984, systematically examined many of the topographical terms contained in the names recorded in Ekwall's *The Concise Oxford Dictionary of English Place-names* (1st edition 1936; 4th edition 1960). Other studies of this nature have been carried out by Anne Cole on, for instance, the meaning of the elements *cumb* and *denu* (Cole 1982), *ora* (1989; 1990) and *mere* (Cole 1993). The majority of these studies have been concerned with topographical features because these can be readily identified in the landscape today. The cumulative efforts on hill features are now well known. Gelling (1984) gives a wide range of meanings for the term *dun* but sees the term most often related to open hill country, not always attaining great heights. She tentatively extends the meaning to include 'series of flat-topped hills suitable for village-sites' (Gelling 1984, 142). But there may be a tendency when dealing with place-names which survived because they became attached to settlements to exaggerate the habitative connection: to me *dun* conveys little more than the sense of 'a whale-shaped hill'. It can be used to refer to a massive hill which dominates the surrounding countryside – again Bredon Hill is an obvious example. Cole would interpret a *dun* feature as 'like an upturned bowl with a limited area of flat land on top' (1989, 15).

On the basis of my experience, I am quite content to believe that there was a theoretical exactness about the use of the Old English terms but I am less certain that it was always adhered to, especially for minor landmarks and at later dates. Two elements referring to barrow-shaped features are British *crug* and Old English *beorg*. Both were obviously in use for both tumuli and tumulus-shaped natural hills. Gelling has argued that the former term was in use for much more pointed hills than the latter and I can only suggest that these arguments are borne in mind when one travels around the countryside.

Remaining for the moment with hill names, the interpretation of *hoh* as 'heel-shaped spur', first suggested by Ekwall, is beautifully portrayed by numerous examples, such as the spur of the ironstone escarpment dominating the parish of Tysoe in south Warwickshire; here the end spur of such a hill has a concave slope before a final small rise reminiscent of an upturned giant's foot (Figure 3.4). An *ora*, on the other hand, is described by Cole as 'more like an upturned canoe or punt having an extensive tract of flat land, often only along one axis, at the summit, terminating at one or both ends with a rounded shoulder' (Cole 1989, 15). But she goes on to suggest that as a Latin loan word it should be viewed against the Roman features in the landscape and points out that 'many an *ora* is beside a Roman or pre-Roman route' or associated with a traditional Saxon landing-place, perhaps a landfall 'at a very early date in the Anglo-Saxon settlement' (Cole 1990, 29). She extends the argument to the Old English term *ofer*, a feature described by Gelling as a 'flat-topped ridge' (Gelling 1984, 173), a term used more frequently in the Midlands and the North. I can confirm that the term occurs in Worcestershire and Warwickshire along a number of saltways which are likely to be ancient routes: Hadzor in Worcestershire lies beside the Roman road and saltway linking Droitwich and Worcester and Haselor in Warwickshire overlooks the Roman road, later known as The Saltway, linking Alcester and Stratford. But I leave readers to judge whether this confirms that the two terms *ora* and *ofer* were only 'used in naming features or settlements along routeways or at harbour entrances', their names 'useful in helping travellers to find their way' (Gelling 1984, 39–41).

Cole has subsequently looked at the Old English term *mere*, a 'body of fresh water, a lake', with special reference to the name *mere-tun*, and has plotted these alongside the Roman road network. In noting a correlation between the thirty examples recorded she has concluded that these were places offering a traveller 'welcome rest and refreshment'. I wonder if there is not a danger here of returning to the Roman road syndrome which occupied so much of place-name scholars' attention when they were first trying to establish a chronology for place-names in general and, incidentally, for dates of boundary demarcation. But there is obviously a great deal of scope for further analysis of the use of place-name terms in the landscape and for those interested in the landscape to go out, armed with their relevant county volume of the English Place Name Society, and consider just how landscape features are described in early forms of many place-names.

The Anglo-Saxon landscape

Early place-names undoubtedly provide us with our surest framework in reconstructing the Anglo-Saxon countryside for so many of them provide clues to the general nature of the landscape at that period. This has been well known for decades but as knowledge of the Anglo-Saxon landscape has increased, so it has become possible for place-names to be used more effectively. Reference has already been made to the changes that were taking place in this period. Unfortunately very little is known about the late Roman countryside, and that information tends to be site-specific, but enough studies have been carried out to show that croplands were shrinking in extent at the end of the Roman period. Agriculture organized on a commercial basis to supply the requirements of towns and the Roman army was virtually abandoned and there appears to have been a return to a more subsistence type of farming at the end of the Roman period. This affected some areas more than others and crop cultivation on the chalk downlands of southern England, for instance, seems to have been withdrawn even from areas exploited for this purpose in Iron Age times.

A build-up of soil pests combined with an element of soil degradation may have been contributory factors in these regions but, whatever the cause, field systems and settlement sites appear to have been abandoned and these often survived as earthworks under pasture or woodland into the present century. Some regions were affected by woodland regeneration more than others but accruing environmental evidence suggests that this must have been a slow process, incomplete even by the end of the Anglo-Saxon period. The role of pastoralism and woodland pursuits will be briefly examined below. With the collapse of wide-scale intensive agriculture, and the increasing concentration on local resources for subsistence farming, wetlands may also have been more greatly appreciated. In the Abingdon area, David Miles (1986) found evidence of fishing and fowling gaining in importance; there is evidence too, that drainage systems in the Fens were not maintained. Fortunately, in the early medieval period there are written sources of evidence for local landscapes for the first time in English history, in the form of charters and their accompanying boundary clauses.

Pre-Conquest charters are documents relating to transfers of land and the granting of privileges attached to land before the Norman Conquest. They often recorded grants to the church or leases by the church to individuals and were preserved in the cartularies of cathedral and monastic libraries. Individuals might also deposit such documents with the church for safe-keeping. Few documents survive in their original form for they were often copied by scribes and several copies kept; most are now in the British Library. These documents provide topographical information in three ways: sometimes the location of a place being granted or leased to another individual is described in enough detail to explain the nature of the countryside of a particular estate; less frequently there are references to agricultural land use on an estate, and, more often, a grant may be accompanied by a boundary clause which describes, usually in Old English, landmarks along the boundary of the estate concerned. In the 1920s and 1930s Grundy (1933–9) did an enormous amount of work upon these boundary clauses but our knowledge of Old English has increased since his day and there is also always scope for more local research into boundary solutions.

I began working on charters in the late 1970s and, as a by-product of other research, worked through the charter-bounds, first, of the West Midlands and, subsequently, southern and south-western England. My suggested solutions for Staffordshire, Worcestershire, Cornwall and Devon are in print – the first published by the University of Keele, the others by the Boydell Press (Hooke 1983; 1990; 1994). Warwickshire will appear shortly and Gloucestershire after that. I, personally, have done as yet only limited work on the charters of Dorset but others have published recent papers on this county, adding to the studies published

Fig. 3.4. Old English terms used to name hill shapes [taken from Hooke's forthcoming book, The Anglo-Saxon Landscape*].*

by Grundy in the 1930s (e.g. Hart 1965). Charter documentation does not exist for the whole country and southern and midland England are best represented: most of the following examples are taken from those areas in which I have had closest experience. The two big drawbacks to charters as a form of historical land-use evidence are, firstly, that they are sporadic in their cover, especially those accompanied by boundary clauses. Some counties like Wiltshire and Worcestershire are very well covered, others much less so, and Dorset is intermediate in charter survival. Second, from their nature, the boundary clauses only refer to landmarks along the boundaries of estate and, unless there is additional information about land use, we are told nothing about activities within the estate itself. Nevertheless a great deal can be inferred, especially when later land-use patterns are reconstructed

How many Anglo-Saxon features can one hope to find in the present landscape? The answer to this must be actually very few that we can positively date. Many of the archaeological features noted in charters were already old when they were described as landmarks and it is perhaps surprising that any survive. Tumuli, for instance, made prominent landmarks along boundaries and have sometimes escaped destruction because of their boundary location or because they lay on heathland or pasture: Welands Smithy is a Neolithic chambered tomb which had acquired its name by the mid tenth century when it was described as a landmark along the boundary of Compton Beauchamp above the Vale of the White Horse (now in Oxfordshire). One can seldom be certain whether the term *beorg* was being used for an actual barrow or to describe a natural barrow-shaped hill. In Devon, for instance, the *hwitan* beorh of Culmstock (Sawyer 1968, S 286; Hooke 1994, 1137–41) may just have been a reference to the prominent knoll of White Ball Hill near the north-western corner of the parish, but on many occasions the named barrows can still be seen today. Iron Age hillforts were also prominent features: along the North Berkshire Downs a number are strung out along a route known as the Ridgeway and several are described in charter-bounds. On the boundary of Uffington, for instance, the eastern boundary passed in 'the north gate of Raven's camp, through the camp, out at the south gate' (Sawyer 1968, S 1208; Gelling 1976, 687). A similar string of forts crown the oolitic limestone escarpment of the Cotswolds: a charter of Willersey refers to the *burhwealles*, the 'fort-wall', where the boundary of Willersey parish follows a rampart of the hillfort (Sawyer 1968, S 1599; Hooke 1990, 408–17). In addition to naming known sites, the charters provide information about many that have failed to survive, like the *haethenan byriggelse*, 'heathen burials', overlooking the Stour valley in Warwickshire (Sawyer 1968, S 1573; Hooke forthcoming b).

Although such sites are of strong archaeological interest all they tell one about the Anglo-Saxon landscape is that they had not then been destroyed by cultivation and probably lay in open land. A second, and by far the largest, group of landmarks refers to the physical features of the locality: rivers and streams, hills and valleys and such like. These again provide only limited information about the use of the countryside. Because such features can be accurately pin-pointed, analysis of the terms used can, however, provide a useful check against mere place-name analysis. Some of the charter *dun* features, for instance, were much less monumental than those which gave rise to the place-names discussed earlier. Just to the east of Ilmington in Warwickshire, two little hills are referred to in a boundary

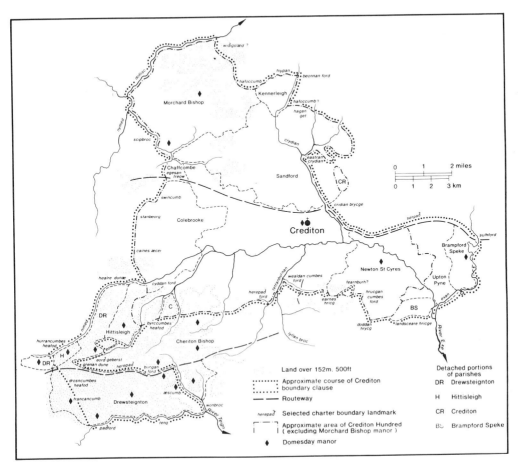

Fig. 3.5. The Pre-Conquest charter of Crediton (Sawyer 1968, S 255).

clause of Longdon in Tredington (Sawyer 1968, S 1321) which are small but prominent features of the shape suggested above. Frequently entire charter-bounds consist of little more than local topographical features. One may ask whether this reflects a locally varied topography or the absence, near the boundaries, of cultivation. The southern boundary of the charter of Crediton in Devon (Sawyer 1968, S 255) for example (Figure 3.5), makes its way across ridges and valleys to the north of Dartmoor and between its journey from the River Exe to the head of the River Teign includes references to one *grenan dun*, 'green hill' (its name surviving as Grendon Down today), five ridges, one of which was described as the 'eagle's ridge', five coombs (one associated with foxes), five streams and seven more fords, a *hlypan* which seems to be a 'leap' across a steep ravine, and a feature described as an *eorthgeberst*, literally an 'earth-burst', which seems to describe another steep ravine near the source of the River Yeo above Treable Woods. Various tree species are mentioned, either as individual trees or as the type associated with particular coombs: thus we find crab-apple, ash, birch, alder and an ivy grove, while the River Yeo may take its name from the yew. As if to draw further attention to the natural landscape and its flora and fauna in this area we also find reference to a wolf-pit which may have been used to trap the animals or was simply a place frequented by wolves; a Grendel's pit may, however, be alluding to the more mythical monster known from the Anglo-Saxon poem *Beowulf*.

The charter boundary clauses clearly show that much of the routeway pattern of medieval England was already in place. Saltways radiating from the inland salt-producing area of Droitwich in the Hwiccan kingdom (now in Worcestershire), for instance, can be traced with considerable precision (Hooke 1981). Similarly, it has been possible to identify many of the early routeways crossing the South West Peninsula.

The nearest charter to Dorset that I have personally worked on in detail is that of Uplyme, a tenth-century grant of King Athelstan (Sawyer 1968, S 442; Hooke 1994, 127–34) (Figure 3.6). In this one finds but brief reference to the 'cliff' which marks the edge of the undercliff although a *sigilmere* on the western boundary may refer to the small rock-bound bay beneath the headland described by the Old English word *sigil*, 'brooch, gem'. Above the cliff was 'the ferny gore' and beyond that 'maple knap'. A 'honey ford' may refer to the presence of wild bees who were sought for their honey, virtually the only sweetening then available, and from that landmark the bounds ran on to 'the sour apple-tree' (a crab-apple). On the heights of the downland one again finds references to barrows and the northern boundary of Uplyme followed a routeway known as the red way. A gallows stood beside this road in the sixteenth century and the charter names a fingerpost called the *crowan staple*, 'crow's post', a little beyond this site. One feature I have not been able to identify is the *sweluende* beside a tributary of the River Lim on the eastern boundary. This term is often translated as 'whirlpool' but means literally 'the swallowing' and the stream here is much reduced in volume during the summer months. Withies and a hazel are noted on the eastern boundary but I am not sure why a lane crossing the boundary was referred to in the 16th century as 'Somersett Lane', from the charter reference here to *somersete*.

Such bounds tell us very little about land use or what was going on within the heart of the estate, but in various papers I have examined charter evidence concerning land use and settlement. Some charters, especially from central and southern England, confirm that open field agriculture had been introduced by the tenth century (Hooke 1988a). In such places as the Vale of the White Horse the areas under cultivation can be identified with considerable precision and shown to have been sloping land above the water meadows but below the turf downland – the same area that remained in cultivation throughout medieval and post-medieval times (Hooke 1988b). References to such features as headlands and acre strips show that cropland reached as far as the boundaries themselves. Such references are particularly frequent when a minor boundary is carving up a pre-existing estate.

Another common term appears to have been associated with hunting regions, often ones which were well wooded. Grundy had few doubts about the interpretation of the term *haga* and gives his considered opinion clearly in a footnote in the Dorset volume: he thought it referred to a game enclosure, as indeed it does in an eleventh-century reference to a deerpark at Ongar in Essex, where Thurstan in his will bequeathed to his page *that wude at Aungre*

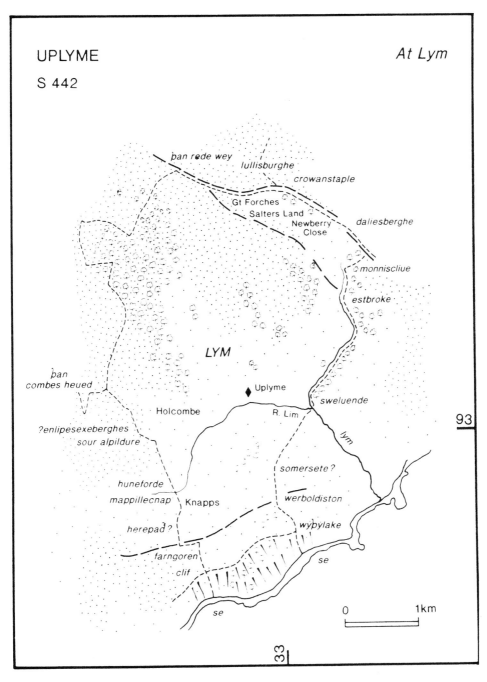

UPLYME
S 442

At Lym

þan rede wey
lullisburghe
crowanstaple
Gt Forches
Salters Land
daliesberghe
Newberry
Close

monniscliue

estbroke

LYM

◆ Uplyme

*þan
combes heued*

sweluende

Holcombe
R. Lim

lym

?enlipesexeberghes
sour alpildure

somersete?

huneforde
mappillecnap Knapps

werboldiston

herepad?

wybylake

farngoren

se

clif

93

se

0   1km

33

Fig. 3.6. The Pre-Conquest charter boundary of Uplyme in Devon.

39

butan that derhage 7 that stod the ic ther habbe, 'the wood at Ongar, except the deerpark and the stud which I have there' (Thorpe 1865, 574). Such a meaning has, however, been rejected by some subsequent scholars and I have had, therefore, to examine the term as critically as possible to seek out its meaning and, above all, to show that this term was distinguishable from other 'hedge' terms. In Germany the term appears to have described on occasions the boundary of a royal forest: a document of AD 801 refers to such features on the boundaries which were to coincide with those of the tenth-century royal forests of Bramforst and Zunderhart (Metz 1954; Hooke 1989). Forests were in existence in the Frankish kingdoms as early as the seventh century (Gilbert 1979, 5). I am confident that the *haga* term was frequently associated with land set aside for hunting either as a reserve or as the boundary of a heath or wooded area. Such a fence might have served a purpose in hunting by forcing driven animals towards netted gaps but was more likely a specially marked-off area like the Domesday *haia*. In the field I have often noted substantial boundary banks which might have supported a timber pale or a dead hedge – probably the latter, because *haga* was also the name for the haw of the hawthorn; the term comes down in some place-names as 'haw'.

In Berkshire *haga* features were common in the south-east of the county and, as elsewhere, their location bears a close relationship to either later deerparks or Norman forests. In northern Hampshire, too, the term as it occurs in pre-Conquest charters is found in areas which seem to have been abandoned for crop growing somewhere around the end of the Roman period and to have been undergoing woodland regeneration during Anglo-Saxon times: indeed, *leah* place-names suggest that there was woodland there by the tenth and eleventh centuries. Earlier agriculture within woodland is clearly indicated by the survival of lynchets, field-systems associated with prehistoric and Roman settlement sites (Hooke 1989).

Many of the landscape regions identified by particular kinds of land use are represented in regions of chalk downland/clay vale country and Dorset is equally well represented. Even a superficial examination of the charter boundary clauses relating to this county permits one to plot the occurrence of terms related to agriculture and those related to woodland. As elsewhere, the *haga* term seems to be one of the key terms representing specific land-use types. In Dorset it appears in a number of areas but is most commonly found in the Vale of Blackmoor (Figure 3.7). This is a region for the most part consisting of heavy clayland. It was a well-wooded region in early medieval times, as was the greensand escarpment which bounded it on the east. Woodland was present on many of the manors recorded in Domesday Book, with substantial quantities recorded on several manors. Much of it was to be declared royal forest, giving rise to the two Norman forests of Blackmoor and Gillingham. Hunting parks granted to manorial lords in medieval times were usually restricted to areas beyond or on the margins of forests and there were, therefore, only a few in the region. They are recorded at Winterbourne Houghton and Duntish in this area of Dorset, with Melcombe Park officially emparked at a later date, and with two others, the park of Gillingham itself and that of Kington Magna, in the north. It is in the central region that we find *haga* features running for long distances along parish boundaries, almost always in association with later woodland. Although the Old English *leah*, indicating wood, is nowhere near as frequent in its occurrence here as in, say, Worcestershire, it is found in the same charter-bounds as the *haga* features, suggesting this perceived link between the *haga* boundary and woodland which may have

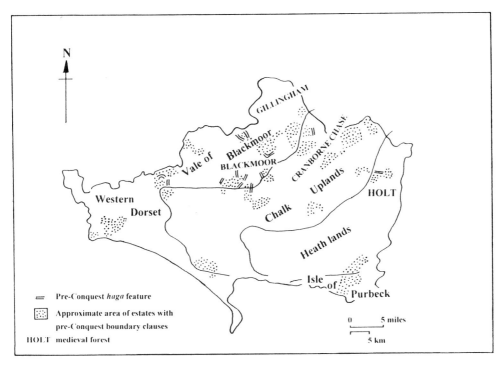

Fig. 3.7. Pre-Conquest haga *features in the county of Dorset recorded in charter boundaries.*

served a specific purpose. Indeed, one Anglo-Saxon *haga* ran along the western boundary of the later Melcombe Park (Figure 3.8). As yet, I have had no opportunity to carry out any fieldwork in the county but I know that this boundary was in the 1960s still represented by a substantial bank (Cantor and Wilson 1964, 145–8). These same estates were also among those which had the largest amounts of woodland recorded in Domesday Book, with one dimension reaching at least a league in Stalbridge, Buckland Newton and Sturminster Newton. Further to the north-east the *haga* recorded along the western boundary of Fontmell is the only one noted on chalk country, but this lay on the western edge of Cranborne Chase. There is clay-with-flints overlying the chalk in this region, in common with much of the *haga* area of north Hampshire, but this particular boundary feature appears to have run along a valley bordering Fontmell Wood on the Middle Chalk in an area where woodland was scattered across a landscape in which there was also much open downland. To the east lay the manor of Ashmore where woodland measuring 2 x 1 leagues is recorded in Domesday Book. The chase itself passed in and out of royal hands in medieval times (Cantor 1982, 73).

Other *haga* features occur along the boundary of Corscombe, in the wooded region fringing the West Dorset region, more specifically where the eastern boundary runs across an outcrop of Oxford clay alongside the woodlands of Chelborough Park; again a park was to be

41

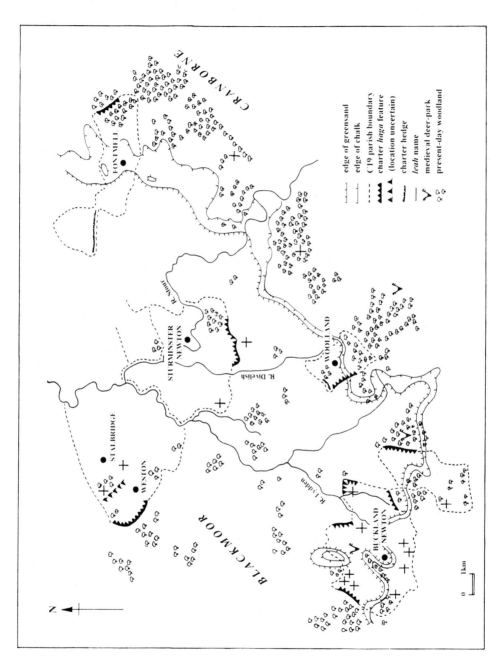

Fig. 3.8. Early woodland features in the Vale of Blackmoor.

enclosed from the waste in West Chelborough, the adjacent parish, in the late 14th century. Most of Dorset's medieval hunting parks lay in this western region. In the north-eastern part of the country there is a similar link-up between *haga* features recorded along the boundary of Horton parish and the Forest of Holt (referred to as a Forest of Wimborne in Domesday Book and assessed with the manor of Horton [Thorn and Thorn 1986, 14,1]). The nearest medieval park lay at Edmonsham in the thirteenth century. Horton parish extends eastwards onto land underlain by the infertile Eocene beds which were to carry most of Dorset's heathland wastes in medieval times.

Although hedges are well represented in the county, and sometimes occur in the same charters as *haga* features, they obviously lay in different locations and it is likely that they enclosed agricultural land. Both terms occur, for instance, in the charter-bounds of Fontmell and Woolland.

The achievements of charter analysis

To summarize, it may be relevant to review some of the achievements of charter analysis. Above all the contribution to the recognition of regional landscapes must be foremost in the geographical use of charters. This is the earliest period for which landscape reconstruction from documentary evidence becomes possible and it reveals the landscape at one of the most formative periods of English history. Not only can the utilization of resources be investigated but this can be related to territorial organization and a rapidly evolving estate network. Such investigation has been helped by the more precise study of the Old English terminology. Even if the features themselves do not survive (and the two Worcestershire landmarks of the title do not), their record provides us with remarkable insight into the Anglo-Saxon countryside and into the landscape regions that are still the basis of present-day landscape character.

Note

1. 'After Rome: Towards an Ethnography of Early Medieval Europe', San Marino, Italy, 27–31 August 1994.

Bibliography

Balkwill, C, 1993, Old English *wic* and the origin of the hundred. *Landscape History*, 16, 5–12

Barker, K, and Seaward, D R, 1990, Boundaries and landscape in Blackmoor: The Tudor manors of Holnest, Hilfield and Hermitage. *Proceedings of the Dorset Natural History and Archaeological Society*, 112, 5–22

Blair, J, 1994, *Anglo-Saxon Oxfordshire*. Stroud. Alan Sutton

Cantor, L M, and Wilson, J D, 1964, The medieval deer-parks of Dorset: III. *Proceedings of the Dorset Natural History and Archaeological Society*, 86 (1963), 141–52

Cantor, L, 1982, Forests, chases, parks and warrens. In L Cantor (ed), *The English Medieval Landscape*. London. Croom Helm. 56–85

Cole, A, 1982, Topography, hydrology and place-names in the chalklands of southern England: *cumb* and *denu*. *Nomina*, 6, 73–87

Cole, A, 1989, The meaning of the Old English place-name *ora*. *Journal of the English Place-Name Society*, 21 (1988–89), 15–22

Cole, A, 1990, The origin, distribution and use of the place-name element *ora*. *Journal of the English Place-Name Society*, 11 (1989–90), 26–42

Cole, A, 1993, The distribution and use of *mere* as a generic in place-names. *Journal of the English Place-Name Society*, 25 (1992–93), 38–50

Copley, G, 1986, *Archaeology and Place-Names in the Fifth and Sixth Centuries* (= BAR British Series 147). Oxford. British Archaeological Reports

Costen, M, 1992, Huish and worth: Old English survivals in a later landscape. In S C Hawkes, J Campbell and D Brown (eds), *Anglo-Saxon Studies in Archaeology and History* 5. Oxford. Oxford University Committee for Archaeology. 65–83

Cox, B, 1975–6, The place-names of the earliest English records. *Journal of the English Place-Name Society*, 8, 12–66

Darby, H C, 1977, *Domesday England*. Cambridge. Cambridge University Press

Dodgson, J M, 1966, The significance of the distribution of English place-names in *-ingas*, *-inga-* in south-east England. *Medieval Archaeology*, 10, 1–29

Ekwall, E, 1936 (4th edition 1960). *The Concise Oxford Dictionary of English Place-Names*. Oxford. Clarendon Press

Gelling, M, 1976, *The Place-Names of Berkshire, Part 3* (= English Place-Name Society Volume LI). Cambridge. Cambridge University Press

Gelling, M, 1978, *Signposts to the Past*. London. Dent

Gelling, M, 1984, *Place-Names in the Landscape*. London. Dent

Gilbert, J, 1979, *Hunting and Hunting Reserves in Medieval Scotland*. Edinburgh. John Donald

Grundy, G B, 1933–39, Dorset charters. *Proceedings of the Dorset Natural History and Archaeological Society*, 55 (1933), 239–68; 56 (1934), 110–30; 57 (1935), 114–39; 58 (1936), 103–36; 59 (1937), 95–118; 60 (1938), 75–89; 61 (1939), 60–78, index.

Hart, C, 1965, Some Dorset charter boundaries. *Proceedings of the Dorset Natural History and Archaeological Society*, 86 (1964), 158–63

Hooke, D, 1981, The Droitwich salt industry: An examination of the West Midland charter evidence. In D Brown, J Campbell and S C Hawkes (ed.), *Anglo-Saxon Studies in Archaeology and History 2* (= BAR British Series 92). Oxford. British Archaeological Reports. 123–69

Hooke, D, 1983, *The Landscape of Anglo-Saxon Staffordshire: The Charter Evidence* (= Studies in Local Archaeology 1). Keele. University of Keele

Hooke, D, 1985a, *The Anglo-Saxon Landscape, the Kingdom of the Hwicce*. Manchester. Manchester University Press

Hooke, D, 1985b, Village development in the West Midlands. In D Hooke (ed), *Medieval Villages: A Review of Current Work* (= OUCA Monograph 5). Oxford. Oxford University Committee for Archaeology. 125–54.

Hooke, D, 1988a, Early forms of open-field agriculture in England. *Geografiska Annaler*, 70B 8 (1), 123–31. Reproduced with corrections in U Sporrong (ed), 1990, *The Transformation of Rural Society, Economy and Landscape*. Stockholm. Department of Human Geography, Stockholm University. 143–51

Hooke, D, 1988b, Regional variation in southern and central England in the Anglo-Saxon period and its relationship to land units and settlement. In D Hooke (ed), *Anglo-Saxon Settlements*. Oxford. Basil Blackwell. 123–52

Hooke, D, 1989, Pre-Conquest woodland: Its distribution and usage. *Agricultural History Review*, 37, 113–29

Hooke, D, 1990, *Worcestershire Anglo-Saxon Charter-Bounds*. Woodbridge. The Boydell Press

Hooke, D, 1994, *Pre-Conquest Charter-Bounds of Devon and Cornwall*. Woodbridge. The Boydell Press

Hooke, D, forthcoming a. Place-names and settlement patterns in west Warwickshire. In D Hooke and D Postles (eds), *Names, Time and Place. Festschrift for R A McKinley*. Leicester

Hooke, D, forthcoming b. *Anglo-Saxon Charter-Bounds of Warwickshire*. Woodbridge. The Boydell Press

Hooke, D, forthcoming c. *The Landscape of Anglo-Saxon England*. London and New York. Leicester University Press

Metz, W E, 1954, Das 'Gehagio Regis' der Langobarden und die Deutschen Hagen-Ortsnamen. *Beitrage zur Namenforschung in Verbindung mit Ernst Dickenmann, herausgegeben von Hans Krahe*, Band 5. Heidelburg. Winter

Miles, D, (ed), 1986, *Archaeology at Barton Court Farm, Abingdon* (= CBA Research Report 50). London. Council for British Archaeology

Robertson, A J, 1939 (2nd edition 1956), *Anglo-Saxon Charters*. Cambridge. Cambridge University Press

Sawyer, P H, *Anglo-Saxon Charters. An Annotated List and Bibliography*. London. Royal Historical Society

Smith, A H, 1956, *English Place-Name Elements* (= English Place-Name Society Volume XXV and XXVI). Cambridge. Cambridge University Press. (2 parts)

Svensson, O, 1992, The *worthy*-names of Devon. *Nomina*, 15 (1991–92), 53–60

Taylor, C, 1983, *Village and Farmstead. A History of Rural Settlement in England*. London. George Philip

Thorn, C, and Thorn, F, 1983, *Domesday Book. 7 Dorset*. Chichester. Phillimore

Thorpe, B, 1865, *Diplomatarium Anglicum Aevi Saxonici*. London. Macmillan

Welch, M, 1983, *Early Anglo-Saxon Sussex* (= BAR British Series 112). Oxford. British Archaeological Reports

4   Historic landscape character mapping in Cornwall

Peter Herring and Nicholas Johnson

Introduction

Pop a pasty in your pocket and walk on past the Hurlers Stone Circles to the early prehistoric hilltop enclosure on Stowe's Hill in the south-eastern corner of Bodmin Moor. All around you, in rough grassland which has provided local farmers with their summer grazing for the last 3000 years, are the visible, familiar and, to a large extent, understandable remains of earlier Bronze Age settlements, fields and ritual monuments. Cutting through and dumped on them are the pits and heaps of tin streamers, miners and granite quarrymen.

This is clearly an historic landscape, it has obvious time depth and has been recorded in detail by landscape archaeologists over the last 15 years (Johnson and Rose 1994). Now look to the south-east towards the Tamar, the silvery threads that separated Saltash from Plymouth, Cornwall from Devon, until the building, in the nineteenth and twentieth centuries, of beautiful rail and road bridges. Between you and them lie medieval churchtowns, hamlets, and solitary farms, joined together by medieval lanes and roads, all embedded in anciently enclosed farmland, its field patterns the products of thousands of years of agricultural history. Dark patches of old broad-leaved woodland have been confined to the ribbons of steep-sided valleys running down to navigable rivers and creeks. Here and there clumps and clusters of more exotic trees betray the positions of great houses within eighteenth- and nineteenth-century ornamental gardens and parklands.

Now travel 40 miles south-west to another Neolithic hilltop enclosure, Carn Brea above Redruth and Camborne. Lean against Lord de Dunstanville's massive granite monument and consider the roofs and parklands of Tehidy, his seat, and below you on all sides, the remains of tin and copper mines, the source of his wealth. Tramways, dressing floors, smelters and counthouses, reclaimed by nature or restored by various heritage agencies, take your eye out towards eighteenth- and nineteenth-century farmland whose straight-sided fields were won from the margins mainly by the families of miners. Away to the west, fringing St Ives Bay, are towans or sand dunes, burying and then revealing prehistoric and medieval farms and fields, and along cliff tops, areas of now neglected coastal rough grazing. The seasonal villages of Cornwall's great modern industry, tourism, stand among them, jealously guarding their busy beaches. A slowly rotating radar dish attracts your attention and turns it towards another aspect of Cornwall's past, national defence: a Second World War airfield at Nancekuke, above Portreath, still used by the modern Air Force.

The whole of Cornwall's land mass – the whole of England's land mass – together with its intertidal zone and navigable rivers, is one historic landscape. The character of every part has been determined or influenced by past human activity and if one looks more closely at the detail visible in the panoramas seen from Stowe's Hill and Carn Brea, the enormous complexity of both the history and the extent of its contribution to the present-day landscape character become apparent.

English Heritage (EH), the Countryside Commission (CoCo), and other bodies with an interest in both understanding the development of the landscape and also in protecting it for the future have become increasingly concerned in the last few years to develop methods of landscape assessment which can bring this historical complexity under some sort of analytical and interpretative control so that the historic dimension of the landscape can be placed alongside such things as landform, vegetation and modern land-use. Such a method needed to go beyond simply identifying archaeologically- or historically-important blocks of the landscape, like, say, south-east Bodmin Moor, or the Stonehenge environs, Worth Matravers' strip lynchets, or the Redruth-Camborne mining district, to produce a systematic assessment of the whole landscape so that the historic character of all parts of the landscape, and the remains which help mould that character, can be fully understood, appreciated, protected and even enhanced. This paper briefly outlines the approach to historic landscape assessment developed and tested by the Cornwall Archaeological Unit.[1]

Towards historic landscape assessment

The Cornwall Archaeological Unit (CAU) had, by late 1993, developed a two-stage method of assessing historic landscape character while working with Land Use Consultants on the Countryside Commission's landscape assessment of the Bodmin Moor part of the Cornwall Area of Outstanding Beauty (AONB) (Countryside Commission 1994). This methodology formed the basis of that refined in 1994 during the Unit's involvement in a county-wide historic landscape assessment undertaken for CoCo and EH in association with the consultancy firm Landscape Design Associates (LDA) who had been commissioned to assess the whole of Cornwall's landscape. The method developed by CAU with advice from LDA and Graham Fairclough of English Heritage was designed with wider application, both beyond Cornwall and also at different levels and scales, firmly in mind. Its success in characterizing and interpreting the historic landscape of a county whose history is particularly rich and varied suggests that the Cornwall approach can be adapted for use in other parts of Britain and Europe.

The CAU method has so far been concentrated on the most visually dominant historic landscape character as its product has been intended for feeding into traditional aesthetics-based landscape assessments. There is, however, no reason why the methods should not be capable of dealing with the landscape at particular key moments in the recent or distant past, given adequate primary sources or confidence in generalising assumptions. Indeed the first steps have been taken towards preparing detailed mapping of Cornwall in the early sixteenth century.

The Cornwall Project involved preparing detailed maps (at 1:25,000 shrunk down to 1:50,000) showing the dominant historic landscape type of every parcel of land in Cornwall. Seventeen separate types were identified in Cornwall:

1. Rough ground – moorland, downland, sand dunes
2. Prehistoric enclosures – predominantly prehistoric pattern
3. Medieval enclosures – predominantly medieval pattern
4. Post-medieval enclosures – predominantly post-medieval pattern
5. Modern enclosures – barbed wire landscapes, areas of massive hedge removal etc.
6. Ancient woodland
7. Plantation
8. Settlements – pre-1900 core
9. Settlements – post-1900
10. Industrial – relict
11. Industrial – active (includes industrial estates)
12. Communications – roads, rail, radio stations etc.
13. Recreation – golf courses, caravan/chalet parks, show grounds etc.
14. Military – airfields etc.
15. Ornamental – parks and gardens, cemeteries, urban parks
16. Water – natural lakes
17. Water – artificial – flooded quarries, reservoirs etc.

If undertaken at larger scales, or with greater resources available, several of the types could have been usefully subdivided; for example 'post-medieval enclosures' can be broken down into wholly new eighteenth- and nineteenth-century farms taken in from previously rough ground, wholly new smallholdings (usually industrial labourers' intakes) and post-medieval adaptations of parts of medieval or prehistoric field patterns.

Numerous systematically-mapped sources were used. The 1:10,000 habitat maps recently prepared by the Cornwall Wildlife Trust from a complete cover of colour aerial photographs taken in 1988 showed areas of rough ground, woodland, dunes and modern intakes, English Heritage and English Nature lists gave details of ancient woodlands and parks and gardens (the latter becoming the ornamental landscapes) and early editions of Ordnance Survey maps indicated the pre-twentieth century cores of historic settlements. Tourist Board publications delineated recreational sites like golf courses and caravan and chalet parks and field patterns were classified according to enclosures' shapes, with earliest documentary references to associated settlements helping to identify medieval and post-medieval farmland.

This first stage of mapping vividly illustrated the fragmented detail of the created landscape and, being the most objective representation of it, formed the raw data used in subsequent stages. Although Cornwall is a large county (3550 square kilometres), this mapping of types was achieved in 60 days and has provided a detailed source which can now be used by all sorts of interested bodies alongside geology, soils and land classification maps etc. In effect, types mapping produces a modern land-use map capable of direct historical analysis, and also capable of periodic updating.

Fig. 4.1. Helsbury, Michaelstow. A later prehistoric hillfort with medieval chapel within an area of Anciently Enclosed Land, part of which (lower left) has been significantly altered by boundary removal in the 20th century [photograph: CAU ACS 4160].

Landscape types to landscape zones

In terms of landscape assessment, however, the historic landscape character types mapping was for most practical purposes considered to be too intricate. Simplifying, generalizing and in some cases interpreting the historical meaning of types led to a second stage of mapping, that of zones or 'super types' producing a much less fragmented and more accessible image (Figures 4.1 – 4.5 illustrate a selection of zones):

1. Anciently Enclosed Land
2. Upland Rough Ground
3. Coastal Rough Ground
4. Dunes
5. Recently Enclosed Land
6. Anciently Enclosed Land extensively altered in the eighteenth and nineteenth centuries
7. Anciently Enclosed Land extensively altered in the twentieth century
8. Navigable Rivers and Creeks
9. Steep-sided valleys

Fig. 4.2. Hurlingbarrow, St Agnes. Recently Enclosed Land, 19th century farms cut out of downland which until then had been Upland Rough Grazing [photograph: CAU ACS 3291].

10. Industrial
11. Urban development
12. Ornamental
13. Recreation
14. Military
15. Airfields
16. Upland woods
17. Reservoirs
18. Inter-tidal zone

Through this, historical processes could be more easily identified, understood and presented. It was also at this level of analysis that typical historical and archaeological components could be recorded and evidence for time-depth and the interaction of both components within individual zones and the zone itself with others could be discussed.

Time-depth matrices were prepared for each of the 18 zones identified in Cornwall to graphically illustrate historical change and efficiently identify typical components. The matrix design was based on that suggested in a recent report on historic landscapes prepared for English Heritage by Cobham Resource Consultants and the Oxford Archaeological Unit

Fig. 4.3. St Agnes Beacon. A small area of Upland Rough Ground with some Anciently Enclosed Land (medieval derived) to its right; Recently Enclosed Land to the left and towards the top. The chalet park (left) is classified as Recreational, and some of the hamlets are large enough to be designated as Settlement. Beyond is a strip of Coastal Rough Ground [photograph: CAU ACS 4169].

(1993) but enhanced by using different symbols to illustrate the principal sources of information. By doing this the matrix identified which sorts of features, from which periods, were most likely to be visible at the surface and therefore contributed directly to present-day landscape character.

Each zone was provided with detailed supporting text, the subsections of which included discussions of the main historical processes which produced the zone and typical historical features found within it. The quality of past historical research on the zone and extent of documentation together with the potential for future research were also outlined. Among subsections considering the condition and future of each zone was one assessing its vulnerability and another making management recommendations intended to protect the zone and sensitively present aspects of it to the interested public.

Both historic landscape character types and zones were utilized alongside professional knowledge and personal preferences in the preparation of a separate and generally less satisfactory mapping of historic landscape character areas, discrete and named blocks of the

Fig. 4.4. Belowda Beacon. An area of Upland Rough Ground with complex remains of prehistoric ritual sites, medieval outfields, and surface tinworking and post-medieval quarrying, with straight-sided fields of Recently Enclosed Land towards the top [photograph: CAU ACS 353].

Cornish landscape for which historical narratives could be prepared. This can perhaps be regarded as the traditional method of mapping the historic landscape but stands out from the CAU two-stage characterization method as being highly subjective. Confidence in its usefulness is to some extent limited to the authority, expertise and prejudices of the historians or archaeologists undertaking the mapping. The main source of uncertainty is in deciding which historical elements or periods of history are the most significant for, firstly, identifying a particular area and then fixing its boundaries in relation to neighbouring areas, the basis of whose identification may be very different. In landscapes where land-use has not been static either spatially or temporally, and where historic landscapes are therefore fluid, making such judgements is fraught with difficulties. The coherence of the historical narratives prepared for the areas is therefore compromised and the preparation of management plans which can be accepted and pursued by local authorities and conservation agencies is very difficult.

All this material – maps, text and tables – was passed on to Landscape Design Associates who assimilated the information into their countywide assessment, alongside that from their more usual sources (geology, hydrology, soils etc) to produce landscape character areas whose boundaries were often defined along the lines of groupings of historic landscape

Fig. 4.5. Lanhydrock. An 18th century designed or ornamental landscape centred on one of Cornwall's largest houses. Previously a deer park and before that a medieval field system occupied the site [photograph: CAU ACS 679].

character zones. Their text, for the first time in an extensive landscape assessment (Cornwall County Council 1996), has also fully incorporated the historic element which is now properly interwoven with landform, vegetation, aesthetics etc. Comments on river catchment areas and exposed coastal plateaux are interspersed with ones on the effects of traditional woodland management or the extent of recently enclosed land and the contribution the bareness and straightness of its field walls makes to the landscape character. More significantly, a full recognition of the great depth of the history of human intervention together with an appreciation of the direction and speed of relatively recent changes has led to much greater awareness of longer-term forces for change in the Cornish landscape and more closely-reasoned recommendations to either control them or to deal with their consequences.

Future work

It is at this stage that the application of the assessment of historic landscapes moves on from the largely academic to the seriously practical. The necessity for the method of assessment to be sufficiently objective and systematic for its product to be accepted, 'owned', and acted upon by those whose responsibilities lie in the management of change and the protection of landscape and all its parts is clearest here.

A full description of the historic character of the landscape of Cornwall is being prepared by the Unit with the assistance of English Heritage. This will form a basic unit or stratum within the County Council's Geographical Information System Environmental Database. It will mesh neatly with the Sites and Monuments Record and the Biological Records database and countywide habitats survey to provide a basic level of landscape description across the whole county. Surely at last the conceptual break-out from site-based myopia?

Note

1. This paper is a slightly altered version of one prepared by Peter Herring for inclusion in a forthcoming English Heritage publication on Historic Landscapes (Fairclough forthcoming). The Historic Landscape Assessment Project was funded by English Heritage, the Countryside Commission, Cornwall County Council and the County's six District Councils.

Bibliography

Cobham Resource Consultants and Oxford Archaeological Unit, 1993, *Historic Landscapes Project. Final Report to English Heritage*. [Circulated typescript report]

Cornwall County Council, 1996, *Cornwall Landscape Assessment, 1994*. Truro. Landscape Design Associates and Cornwall Archaeological Unit

Countryside Commission, 1994, *The Landscape of Bodmin Moor* (Report by Land Use Consultants and Cornwall Archaeological Unit). Cheltenham. Countryside Commission

Fairclough, G, forthcoming, *Yesterday's Landscape, Tommorrow's World*. London. English Heritage

Johnson, N, and Rose, P, 1994, *Bodmin Moor. An Archaeological Survey. Volume 1: The Human Landscape to c1800* (Historic Buildings and Monuments Commission for England Archaeological Report 24 / RCHME Supplementary Series 11). London. Cornwall Archaeological Unit; Historic Buildings and Monuments Commission for England; Royal Commission on the Historical Monuments of England

5 'A trifle historical': Making landscapes in Northumbria

Peter Fowler

Prologue

More than a generation has passed since a young Chris Taylor ventured in the early 1960s into an unknown Dorset – for all he knew about it, full of serpents, wolves and curious natives. He was not unpleased with what he saw, however, especially when after a few years' wanderings over curving down and dusty byway he was able to share his enthusiastic insights into a gentle landscape through his own book published somewhat in advance of that of his employers. His audience was then a new one, in size and expectancy if not in nature or age. It was the new leisured and educated middle class emerging from the post-war world in some number on the back of universal education, reasonably full employment and a dawning sense that life could indeed begin at 40 rather than fade as the nest emptied. It was a world of expectancy, of some hope and vision and of Extra-Mural classes where, before the end of the decade, archaeology and local history had taken over from economics as the topic most in demand and most widely provided. Britain was apparently on the brink of at last becoming a civilized place, and then it all started to go horribly wrong. Unconsciously – but perhaps not? – *The Making of the English Landscape* series reflected this deep social change, for in some ways the two Taylor volumes (1970; 1973) marked its zenith.

Introduction

Sadly for a Northumbrian and, indeed, for a less chauvinistic perception of England's northernmost county, *The Northumberland Landscape* (Newton 1972) was not up to the prevailing standards of the time when it was published. I remember feeling terribly disappointed as, from a distance, I tried to renew acquaintance with a boyhood landscape through another's words, only to recognize in them worthy local history rather than the Hoskinsonian vision then imbuing research in Wessex and the West Country. Even at the time, *Northumberland* stood out as a weak member of *The Making of the English Landscape* series doubly graced by Chris Taylor, pioneering in Dorset and then more maturely in Cambridgeshire (Taylor 1970; 1973).

Those Taylor *oeuvres* bracketed the appearance of *Northumberland*, unknowingly highlighting its deficiencies. Despite his background in geography, even Taylor could not have written the sort of *1066 and All That* howler perpetrated by Newton: for example ... 'it was the Anglian farmers, clearing the heavier soils for the plough, who did most to eradicate the original tree-cover, and to set in motion a process which ended in the denuded landscape of the early eighteenth century' (Newton 1972, 31). Though we may still debate when tree-felling for land-clearance began, the idea that the process was 'set in motion' in the sixth century AD now comes as rather a jolt. I seem to recall that that sort of simplistic approach was already superseded when *Northumberland* was in the writing. In checking biblio-graphically whether my criticism is justified, however, I am struck by the number of key studies which were published in the decade 1973–83 and therefore unavailable to Newton. Still, at least *The Northumberland Landscape* made two signal points merely by being published and by being in the *English Landscape* series: that Northumberland, the county, exists, and that it is in England.

It is still a common perception, especially south of Watford, in the metropolitan media and within the tourist trade, that Hadrian's Wall is the boundary between England and Scotland. It is not, and a lot of history has gone into producing that fact. Yet, so it is also wrongly assumed, this erroneous item of landscape history is further seen as continuing today the state of affairs 1900 years ago. North of the Wall are in fact two thirds of Northumberland, filling the unconceptualized 'blank', roughly 70 miles long and 20–40 miles wide (*c.* 115 by 45 km), between Tyne and Tweed. There is more, of Northumberland that is: an equally unknown third of the county lies south of the Wall, in the northern Pennines. In landscape terms, this is quite a lot of nothingness not to have a history.

Though most of my 'Northumbrian' here is in the sense of the county of Northumberland, there are also several larger 'Northumbrias'. An historical one, for example, is Bede's early Anglian kingdom, *provinciae omnes Northymbryorum*, stretching north to the Firth of Forth from the River Humber. A present-day one embraces the territorial remit of the Northumbria Tourist Board. They come into the picture too, but 'Northumbrian' here means 'of Northumberland' unless otherwise indicated.

Newton's (1972) Northumbrian book was conceived, written and published, like Hoskins' and Taylor's throughout, in positivist mode. They all unconsciously assumed, though never argued, that there was a discernible, identifiable landscape out there for the describing, that it was in the singular, and that it had been made once or at least, however episodically, within a linear, chronometric sequence. Hence the use of the definite article throughout: *The Making* (singular) *of the English Landscape* (singular again): *The Northumberland Landscape* (singular yet again). I do not wish to labour the point further and perhaps seem a killjoy, for the series has given enormous pleasure and guidance to so many including, especially, this writer. Nevertheless, a 25 year Taylor-made celebration is bound to involve some appraisal too, and it would be perverse not to recognize that those beloved books were written in more confident but less sophisticated times than the clever but doubting 1990s.

It is a worrying thought, and sad too, that the book that Newton should have written 25 years ago cannot now be written. Even the landscape of the great Northumbrian blank – damn, I too have now fallen into the singular trap – is many-layered, not just physically and through time, as in the models of geologists and archaeologists, but in conceptions and perceptions as in the models of geographers, sociologists, and tourist persons. We are now in a world, nevertheless, where Hoskins' basic thesis that the landscape is man-made has, to all intents and purposes, been accepted in non-academic fields as axiomatic. Paradoxically, however, in places where they think, basic questions are being asked. 'What is a landscape?', for example, 'How extensive does a landscape have to be to become one?'. Further, 'How does all this emphasis on man-made-ness fit with current concerns with the green revolution and a benignly-powerful Nature?'. Yet again, 'What price a model of Man-within-Nature if the former is forever imposing himself on the latter as something separate?'.

And deeper still lurks the question, not just 'Who made the landscape?' but 'Who owns the landscape?'. At one level, in Northumberland, that is a very easy question to answer in general, for the Duke, principally through Northumberland Estates, and half a dozen other major landowners legally hold title to the land in a county which persists as one of the last great bastions with more than a hint of feudal tenure – an interesting survival with major consequences for the history and present appearance of the landscape. Yet in Northumberland, as elsewhere, not only are there a whole range of perceptions of those landscapes but also a broad spectrum of stakeholders who would, in one way or another, 'own' at least part of it.

This is most marvellously illustrated along Hadrian's Wall. Doubtless the corporate messages add much to the confusion of visitors who, on the whole, are probably indifferent to the name or status of whichever institution it is that looks after what the public regards as its 'own' anyway. Along the road, and at key points where people gather, they witness in effect a visual slanging match between signs and 'information boards' from different organisations, all essentially vying for a stake in the Glory that was Rome and, now, in the numinosity of a World Heritage landscape. It is a landscape which historically owes nothing to any of them and everything to those who have previously actually owned and used the place. It is quite an interesting thought, if you think about it in the heritage-conscious 1990s, that, in general, today's publicity-conscious institutional managers of heritage have seldom made any significant contribution to the processes which have produced that very historicity which they now seek to manage. Especially is that true of landscape: 'Whose landscape?' have we in mind indeed when we talk about an 'historic' one and write about its 'making'?

Certainly I, and I suspect Christopher Taylor too, would have had little truck with such questions. What is this academic hair-splitting? What is its point? – philosophical niceties, Hoskins-theoretical issues and heritage management, none of them do anything other than muddle our clear vision of that which we are all about. The landscape is there and we can see it; it has a history, we can interpret it and we tell it as well as we can. The historic (or historian's) landscape is now, however, only one of several which are perceived to occupy the space filled with *terra firma*. Indeed, even that one is now recognized as more a cultural overlay on, a particular perception by particular people of, the geology, geomorphology, physical geography and flora occupying an area of terrestial space. This particular perception is concerned not so much with what is there as with what has happened there to produce what the historian sees.

Henry Tegner (1970, chapters 1 and 2), one of the few even mildly distinguished Northumbrian writers, saw his Cheviot country as first 'mainly geological' and, only second 'a trifle historical'. It could not be expected that such a perspective of landscape would include the archaeological one indicated below. That one, old but conceptually new and perceptually modern, is a sort of landscape invisible to Tegner and many a countryside-writer both before and since (*cf.* Fowler 1995); but presumably it was there nevertheless 25 years ago, unless our archaeological dating is very wrong indeed. In other contexts a forester or property developer would see the same landscape differently again, respectively for its silvicultural potential and financial return; others no longer even limit their perception of landscape to earthbound views, as for example with electronic landscapes (Morley and Robins 1995). The age of the virtual landscape is upon us and landscape history must come to terms with that.

Meanwhile, back in the 'real' landscape ...

Making the historic Northumbrian landscape

What follows is a brief outline of some facets of what could, in the late 1990s, contribute to a conventional 'Hoskinsonian' version of a history of the Northumbrian landscape. It stops as documentary evidence begins to become significant, a most un-Hoskinsonian thing to do but enforced here for purely practical, non-conceptual reasons. It is preceded by a note on some sources, the purpose of which is merely to indicate, mainly for outsiders unfamiliar with a little-known county, the sorts of material available for a fuller study. This little 'source-exercise' is primarily to indicate a personal belief that numerous histories of landscape lie within the discernible landscape, and that Northumberland's physical landscape contains, not just fine sights and wonderfully-preserved sites, but a finely-meshed series of cultural landscapes of considerable significance.

The county enjoys a fine tradition of antiquarian scholarship, enshrined in the *History of Northumberland* which made a Victoria County History redundant. It also contains plentiful primary evidence, some of it of far more than local significance. The documentary and field evidence of the vicissitudes of the 'national' frontierland between England and Scotland, for example, relates to a broad and long-running topic. Some of the archaeological evidence is also of considerable significance. Obviously, this is true of Hadrian's Wall, now officially recognized as such internationally in being at the core of the 'Roman Military Zone' World Heritage Site. Less obviously, the Museum of Antiquities, Newcastle University, primarily known for its Roman collections, also contains Northumbrian material of significance for British prehistory, notably late Neolithic and early Bronze Age pottery, and later Bronze Age metalwork (Tait 1965; Burgess 1968; Gibson 1978).

Northumberland's outstanding characteristic in this context, however, almost certainly still to be exploited scientifically, lies in its field archaeology, especially its earthworks of prehistoric date. The quality of some of this evidence is very high. It includes, for example, not just considerable extents of ancient landscapes analogous to (but distinctly different from) the better-known ones on Dartmoor and Bodmin Moor; its detail includes patches of 'cord rig' with the slightest of rigs clearly overlying one another. It is not uncommon to find palisade-trenches and individual postholes clearly delineated in the Cheviot grass. This sort of landscape, however, hardly figures outside the knowledge and specialist writings of those who study it. As a result, popular perception of one sort of historic landscape reality has barely advanced beyond Newton's 23-year old simplicity quoted above.

Such would indeed appear to be the case if correctly exemplified by a classic synthesis dismissing Northumbria's prehistory in one sentence: 'The history of Northumbria begins with the first groups of settlers in their circular huts and scooped enclosures, making a precarious living on the foothills of the Cheviots and Cleveland Hills. The Romans ...' (Frazer and Emsley 1989, 17). On the other hand, could this be bettered? The environment in which we now live is not of our making, nor the making of our parents' or grandparents' generations, but represents the sum of human activities within the region since the first wandering parties of hunters and food-gatherers penetrated the coastal plain and the river valleys perhaps 10,000 years ago. Our present landscape includes elements accumulated over this long time-span (McCord 1991, 1). Part of the recent blame for a failure to build on that sort of landscape concept with detailed investigation leading to improved academic understanding and then informed popular synthesis must lie, strangely, with the Royal Commission on the Historical Monuments for England. It completed, but has not published, a detailed study of part of the Cheviot landscape which could change perceptions and, in coming from so prestigious a body, give weight to new ideas. Although the data is in the public demesne in the sense that it can be consulted – and indeed they have been used by others, for example Northumberland County Council – this is not quite the same as having to hand a synthesis and discussion, as is now the case with Bodmin Moor (Johnson and Rose 1994). The fact that, for her 1995–6 dissertation, one of my third year students has chosen to analyze the settlement evidence of Bodmin Moor and not of Cheviot country makes the point.

Northumberland meanwhile has indeed been covered reasonably well elsewhere, either as a county, or topically or by period, or as part of northern England (e.g. House 1969; Clack and Gosling 1976; Atkinson 1977; Chapman and Mytum 1983; Musgrove 1990). One of the best studies remains Tomlinson (1888), while among more recent books Sharp (1937), Miket and Burgess (1984), and Frazer and Emsley (1989) stand out. With due respect to Beckensall (1992), however, the county crucially lacks a modern, authoritative study of its place-names. There are of course legions of derivative 'popular' accounts about the country or parts of it, not least about Hadrian's Wall. This author is himself party to a county mini-guide, insubstantial maybe but at least with the merit not shared by all similar-looking guide-books of being based on a first-hand acquaintance with the county and its historical evidence in the field (Boniface and Fowler 1989). Nowhere, however, has Northumberland been treated in a major, successful, multi-period, interdisciplinary synthesis. The nearest approach to that is, now, Pevsner's *Northumberland* in its second edition (Grundy 1992), with its authoritative surveys of various topics about the county in addition to a mass of new data about individual historic buildings. The Royal Commission has made some amends in this field with an excellent survey of buildings under threat on Tyneside (RCHM 1990). Most are of the nineteenth and twentieth centuries, items of the urban industrial heritage which somehow does not seem to attract the same attention as the more romantic but often economically marginal sites constituting the material of industrial archaeology in the countryside.

The post-glacial landscape of Northumberland has been continually volatile, a landscape tradition which continues actively in the present. The long east-facing coast, for example, with its miles and miles of sedimentary rocks, sands and dunes, both changes daily and is subject to long-term change from the effects of both people and Nature. People, wind and water move sand around continuously. Tides continually work away at the nearest toe of land exposing Mesolithic flints, prehistoric land-surfaces and sharply-coloured sections of geomorphological accumulation and denudation. Wind and water have buried lengths of Second World War concrete block-and-hawser defences while upending contemporary pill-boxes among the dunes. Open-cast coal-mining has gutted huge tracts of countryside both inland and just behind the dunes, its depredations now in part disguised in a new landscape of recreational conservation. Such exploitation could prove hardly to have begun if some of the economic forecasts prove correct, for rich and thick carboniferous deposits lie attractively near the surface of a significant area of Northumberland's landscape. The further evolution of that landscape is certain.

A chronological view of prehistoric evolution would see major, successive 'makings' of that landscape, beginning with Mesolithic communities modifying the flora rather than the physical geography. A conventional view would see a fourth millennium BC landscape dominated by forest, of alder-rich woodland along the rivers and other wetlands and mixed deciduous woodland over much of the rest of Northumberland. Major uncertainties exist about the extent to which this tree-coverage was a mosaic of natural and anthropogenic clearings, and thereafter, from about 3000 BC, the rate at which it was further broken up. Nevertheless, probably during the third, and then again during the second and first millennia BC, we can envisage surges of development forming the basis for a likely model for landscape change rather than a steady, linear development fuelled by agrarian progress. In a county then, as now, with an altitudinal difference from sea-level to mountain top of some 700m, generalization must always be tempered by allowance for topographical variability. Palynological data from high on what are now the county's western moorlands, for example, are not necessarily indicative of what was happening on the coastal plain.

This factor is not, of course, peculiar to Northumberland but it is a real one all the same in locating and interpreting landscape evidence there. Early Neolithic settlement, for example, is difficult to perceive, and long barrows are rare, but clearly the Milfield Basin formed a major node of activity from the middle Neolithic onwards (Miket 1976; 1981; Harding 1981; Waddington 1997). Nevertheless, one of the major landscape enigmas is the apparent absence of the settlements of those who created Northumbria's outstanding and prolific 'megalithic art' (Beckensall 1983). Settlements are, however, known from within the second millennium, especially from its later centuries when much of at least the upland landscape was in extensive use. It is from then that some of Northumberland's finest field archaeology exists, as earthworks of settlements, fields and cairnfields on the slopes of Cheviot and the upper, western end of valleys like Coquetdale and College Valley (Miket and Burgess 1984). The most exhaustive study and analysis of these second millennium BC (and later) landscapes has taken place at this northern edge of Northumberland and to the north across into Scotland (Mercer and Tipping 1994). The Breamish Valley is currently the scene of further work, including excavation, by Durham University (Archaeological Services 1996).

If it is accepted that, for whatever reason, an upland-centred phase of landscape development closed in the later part of the middle Bronze Age, around 1100 BC, then another major archaeological horizon long associated with the work of George Jobey can be seen as separate and new from about the seventh century. The Royal Commission's aerial photographic-based survey has embraced the eastern Cheviots slightly further south, including large tracts of grassland and valley bottoms, and would doubtless throw light on this fairly major issue in the making of Northumberland's landscape. Further south, though on a much smaller scale, a detailed examination of Hartington Moor, an areas of burns (streams), bogs, mixed grass and heather on the Wallington estate by this author and others, is currently producing, in a familiar experience, a previously unnoted landscape of cairns, fields, settlement enclosures and open settlements. An early structural phase might well begin in the second millennium BC but most of the field evidence suggests the development of a more ordered landscape in the first millennium BC (Fowler 1986–8). The Hartington Moor data might fit such a model of late Bronze Age discontinuity including its incapacity at the moment to throw light on what was happening between the end of the second and the middle of the first millennia BC. A landscape continuum of Bronze Age into early Iron Age is currently difficult to see, though it is probably there, hidden perhaps among the thousands of Northumbrian cairns (field clearance and otherwise).

In the field, again very much on hills and valley slopes, superbly preserved suites of enclosed settlements, fields, often now with cord-rig, and linear boundaries survive from the later two-thirds of the first millennium BC (Topping 1989). Often, as mentioned above, they exhibit extraordinary detail. Nor is such evidence confined to the higher land: the landscape seems to have filled up to some extent in later prehistoric times, for settlements and agrarian earthworks exist also on lower ground where medieval and later farming has been non-intensive. The now rough-grazing land of the Wallington estate mentioned above, for example, is only about 230m above sea level but significantly it appears to embrace the marginal land between permanent arable and permanent pasture. Despite the good preservation of prehistoric and Roman period earthworks, this status is strongly suggested by sporadic areas of medieval and later ridge and furrow and by evidence of peat-digging. Elsewhere, enclosed and unenclosed settlements, alone and with a variety of field systems, have been noted, by fieldwork, by air photography and in excavation, across the mixed-farming area of middle Northumberland – basically a long south-north strip either side of the Great North Road (A1) between Newcastle and Berwick. Although Cobbett referred to part of this zone, between Morpeth and Alnwick, as 'a country without people', research continues to fill in a picture of greater land-use there in later prehistoric and Roman times than the scarcity of visible earthworks would suggest (exemplified in McCord 1991; air photography by N McCord and T Gates, prints in aerial photographic collection at the Museum of Antiquities, Newcastle University).

Nevertheless, Milfield and parts of the Tyne Valley apart, there is at present no overwhelming amount of evidence to indicate large-scale valley clearance and settlement until the Roman period (and some would say, with Newton 1972, until after that period). As a busy and significant imperial frontier zone periodically over three centuries or more, however, Northumberland's landscape would surely have been markedly affected then. Indeed, the imperial mark can still be seen not only in the ruins of the military establishments, not only in the frequent recycling of their materials into farm and field wall now so characteristic of the landscape, but also, arguably, in the landscape itself. How much of the treeless character of the Wall's central length, for example, is pre-mural and how much today is due to intensive Roman usage? Countless generations of grazing sheep may well have continued, rather than caused, a break in the natural cycle of regeneration. Thanks almost entirely to Jobey (for his bibliography, see Miket and Burgess 1984, 411–14), we know a great deal about the morphology and distribution of civilian settlement to set beside the *magna opera* of the Roman military and its students, but the environmental dimension and its dynamics across the range of Northumbrian topographies in the first millennium AD have still to be taken forward from the stage of revealing but tantalizingly incomplete pioneer research (Turner 1983). Similarly, a major step forward was recently taken in understanding the products of the landscape with the publication of van der Veen's research (1992) on crops and associated palaeo-flora in north-east England, and it is to be hoped that her relatively small sample of sites will now be enlarged by someone encouraged by such pioneering work.

The environmental generalization in the preceding paragraph deliberately extends beyond the Roman period for, despite the glow of Northumbria's Golden Age, either side of AD 700, the post-Roman landscape – that is as a construct of historians – is still there for the making. Morris (1977) has bravely attempted to establish a tenurial framework for a little later but otherwise we are left with a noticeable irony here. Northumbria is, of course, perhaps at its best-known politically, religiously and artistically at this early medieval period, but the landscape, the environmental context, in which this flowering occurred turns out to be, on detailed examination, not known well at all. That would not have mattered very much of course when history was indeed synonymous with politics, religion and cultural achievement. Now, it is a measure of the way in which the sense of history has been extended, in part through the influence of W G Hoskins and his acolytes, that it is perfectly legitimate to point to such a gap in our historical knowledge (*cf.* Higham 1986).

There now comes a conscious gap in this brief coverage. Neither Hoskins nor Taylor would have approved of stopping our landscape-making around AD 700, but that we must do here despite the obvious fact that, in Northumberland of all places, the next 1200 years are important and reasonably well-known. We can but nod in the direction of castles and great estates, of a frontier long fought over, of widely admired agrarian innovations 200 years ago and major industrial and urban development over the last two centuries – it is these which have very much given us the main visual characteristics of the Northumbrian landscape today (House 1969; Atkinson 1977; Musgrove 1990; RCHM 1990; McCord 1991). But now we want to move to the present, and some makings of landscape still in progress.

Making up landscapes

Landscapes often feature in people's imagination, as novel after novel illustrates, but some seem to find it desirable, perhaps even necessary, to make their landscapes of the mind physically exist. As remarkable as the range of landscapes are the many motivations. The real Northumbrian landscape well exemplifies the genre of fantasy landscape and its makers, a phenomenon just worth mentioning here, though its exposition requires more space elsewhere.

Let us simply note a dozen varied examples. Northumbria contains several reconstructions – perhaps 'restoration' is a more appropriate word? – of authentic archaeological structures. The best-known – though not always recognized as such – are various lengths of Hadrian's Wall, restored and consolidated by several bodies over the last century and a half. A prehistoric equivalent is Blawearie burial cairn above Old Bewick, first excavated by Canon Greenwell and then again, with subsequent restoration, by Beckensall in the mid-1980s. Motivation in such cases was undoubtedly well-meant. The same is true of some, but not all, new creations, often wrongly called 'reconstructions', based on authentic originals. Again *Romanitas* has greatly and understandably lent its weight to such, notably at *Vindolanda* with its off-site replicas and *Arbeia* with its on-site, life-size model of a gateway. Recently, a full-size replica of a length of Hadrian's Wall, as it was, was built right beside the foundations of the real thing in Wallsend.

Iron Age houses are also in vogue; one is in hand in east Newcastle for educational purposes and another, mere decoration on a diversifying farm and now rather sad, sags in the fields near an abandoned RAF airfield in eastern Northumberland. Much more proudly 'prehistoric' is the splendid megalithic structure uprightly marking the royal opening of Keilder reservoir. Its parentage would appear to lie in what was doubtless felt to be opportunistic appropriateness deriving from twentieth-century folk memory rather than in a cultural continuity over the millennia in a county-wide landscape actually sparsely furnished with things megalithic. The Keilder one has no apparent specific analogue; but it is impressive.

A much softer imprint, the emphasis on protection, interpretation and infrequent appropriate use, can be seen at Ebba's Chapel, Beadnell, on the coast. It lies on a rocky promontory, Ebb's Nook, usually windy and often gale-lashed. There, detailed field survey (Fowler 1992; 1993) followed by careful consideration had, by 1995, led to various steps being taken by the County Council to minimize erosion, tidy up the interior of the chapel and engage people's interest with an attractive graphic interpretation of the chapel's appearance, setting and significance in early Christian and medieval times.

Not entirely dissimilar in intent is the road-side presentation at 'Heavenfield', Wall, with its large explanatory information board about real historical events and characters; but the whole is much more of a fantasy in the sense that the actual site of the battle, though doubtless somewhere within a few miles, is not precisely known and is indeed difficult to pin down from the topographically ambiguous documentary evidence (Eagles 1993).

Nevertheless, undoubtedly this is an area of historic landscape either side of the demolished Hadrian's Wall. To the immediate north is the living church of St Oswald, just possibly, as legend would love it to have been, on the spot where Oswald as Christian king planted a cross as focus of his followers' prayers before the battle. Alternatively, the present church is possibly on the site where, as Bede tells us, the Hexham monks 'recently' constructed a church. Be that as it may, the lonely building in its leafy, walled churchyard unquestionably adds ambience to a holy and historic place.

This quality is apparently underlined by a large wooden cross. Standing just south of the line of the Wall, it acts as a real eye-catcher right beside the modern road (here on top of

General Wade's mid eighteenth-century Military Way). In fact the cross is a spurious addition to this landscape's historicity. Far from it being either old in itself or marking a traditional site of worship, the cross is a relic of a briefly-successful 1930s attempt by the local vicar to create a place of pilgrimage (Eagles 1991). 'Re-create' might be more accurate, for we have been reminded recently that 'The brethren (at Hexham) initiated (in Wilfred's time) the custom of an annual pilgrimage to the battlefield on Oswald's death-day...' (A Thacker in Stancliffe and Cambridge 1995, 107; many of the academic issues clustered around St Oswald and Heavenfield are learnedly discussed in the same volume, but throughout on the assumption that the modern cross and isolated church unambiguously mark the actual site of the battle in 634).

In a sense an attempt by the Forestry Commission to create an interesting walk in Keilder Forest by inventing the 'Reivers' Trail' also hinges on the invention of a well-meaning but nevertheless fantasy landscape. Its main ingredients are truly real and historic; the remains of bastles and pele-towers, exposed rather than consolidated, well-researched and explained in excellent information panels. Such fairly unattractive ruins are themed along a trail inviting people to undertake a walk on the wild side in present-day Northumberland while encouraging them to imagine the rough and tumble, the insecurity, of life in a medieval landscape without conifers. This seems successfully to meet present-day demands for access, not just to countryside for recreation but to landscape for imagination.

Maybe fantasy is less overt along Newcastle's Quayside in the 1990s, but it might conceivably be dangerous. There a major investment in a new commercial, residential and cultural development is taking place. Its planning respects the axes of medieval *chares* (narrow lanes, alleys) and property boundaries stretching back from the newly reinforced river frontage; the spectacular edifice of the early twentieth-century concrete Co-op is duplicated, not just respected. But what about the historical verity underlying this well-intentioned effort to restore life and liveliness to the riverfront? The Quayside of history and indeed recent memory bustled and hummed because it had a real function; ships tied up there to be loaded and unloaded. Now, riverside Newcastle as a port is dead, its riverscape is empty for want of a trading ship. The Quayside has lost its sole *raison d'être*, and nothing the architects and planners can do can recreate that genuine mercantile liveliness. They may of course succeed in bringing life back to the riverside, their self-avowed aim, and such life would be welcome; but it must surely be developed and recognized for what it is, a late twentieth-century pastiche of eclecticism which can only work on its own terms and not nostalgia. Otherwise, instead of mild fantasy merely embellishing a vigorous new development with a life and justification of its own, from the start an historical misunderstanding about a non-returnable life could well dog with disappointment the twenty-first-century workings of a fantasy-based 1990s landscape.

Just a few miles up river, meanwhile, the Gateshead Metro Centre has no such qualms about the viabilities of the historic landscapes made within it. There are two of them (discounting 'The Mediterranean village' which, while making considerable demands on chauvinistic cliché, fortunately makes no claims on historicity). They are brash and vulgar creations, with no pretence to accuracy, conceived and designed solely as vehicles for retail trade with a consumerist society. That they are so tatty, so pathetically hackneyed, probably tells us, like all good landscapes, more about their makers than their inhabitants. One, called The Forum, displays a sort of sawn-off classicism in the truncated verticality of its hollow, polystyrene columns.

Creating a landscape of AD 700 in the 1990s: *Gyrwe*, Bede's World

Bede's World lies in Jarrow, South Tyneside; it is also of the mind.

The essence of experiment in field archaeology is simplicity. Straight away, therefore, a question must arise about a proposal to experiment in early medieval farming; how valid can it be if, to proceed, complexity has to be reduced to simplicity? Butser Ancient Farm, Hampshire (Reynolds 1979) has provided some answers, theoretically and empirically. The farming aspects of the Bede's World project are well aware of the 25-year experience of Iron Age farming on Wessex chalk, scientifically and also of farming in the public gaze for educational and income purposes. Compared to the arcadia of the Hampshire/Sussex border, Jarrow on Tyne is a different country. Indeed, it lies in Catherine Cookson Country, and we have to do some things differently there, but nevertheless our stance is the practice of presenting a worthwhile experience for visitors based on principles of scholarship, authenticity, discovery and involvement.

Butser began as a seriously experimental ancient farm and then had to accommodate the public's interest. Bede's World is immediately different. The project's prime motivation is veneration for a great (local) man. It is also very much inspired by the thought of achieving that aim by creating an educational centre and international visitor attraction, including a beautifully conceived large, new museum building, in an environmentally upgraded setting in the post-industrial landscape of South Tyneside.

The early medieval farm is but an element within that conceptual framework, but it is an important one. At the moment, certainly, its immediate prime function is as a visitor attraction, for the finances of the project demand that visitor numbers rise now while the project develops, funds assemble, and buildings are constructed. Serious experiment is therefore as yet minimal and not a major priority, but since we have to plough the fields, sow and harvest, and keep animals which visitors love to see, a tentative beginning has been made. We have in any case learnt a lot merely by starting and having to face such basic questions as 'What sort of arable field would Bede have looked out on?' and 'How and with what did his brethren cultivate it?' It is amazingly disconcerting to be looking at an empty chunk of landscape, cleared of its industrial debris, and have to answer such questions knowing that, with the power of modern machinery and an obliging civil engineer, you can have whatever sort of Anglo-Saxon landscape you care to define.

Gyrwe, the OE original of Jarrow, was first resuscitated and then applied to the new 'old landscape' physically created in 1992–3 on some 12 acres of former petrol storage tank farm. Then, obviously, the landscape had to be provided with various features to meet statutory requirements – access for a fire-engine and ambulance, for example – and to enable it to meet its intended function of receiving visitors. The principal archaeological/ historical elements defined for inclusion were timber buildings, fields, trackways, a ford, a stream and a pond, set in a valley landscape with wooded slopes. They presented some problems individually, but the real issues arose over their spatial relationships and their dynamics, for basic to the whole concept was the intention to make this landscape work. We knew we did not have enough land to replicate a complete early medieval agrarian system, but we wanted to demonstrate the workings of elements within such, not merely exhibit a static display.

To that end, the valley slopes were planted with some 10,000 trees and shrubs, all of species known to have been growing in Northumbria around AD 700 and none of them later introductions. Millions of appropriate flower seeds were also sown. We have acquired unimproved or nearest equivalent stock, various breeds of sheep, cattle, pigs and geese, all also visitor attractions and faecal contributors to our attempt to kick-start Mother Nature into agrarian life in unpropitious circumstances. We have experienced, however, a combination of very poor soil, severe drainage problems and extremes of weather as normal in 1993–5, notably bitterly cold Mays and long, very dry periods, especially in 1995. This has severely inhibited tillage and plant growth and it has not yet been possible to see the development of either the botanical aspects of the farm or to begin a serious experimental programme. Beginning with tiny amounts of ancient cereal seed bought from Butser, however, we have moved through three successful harvests (1993, 1994, 1995) to a position of self-sufficiency in our arable seeds, namely in einkorn, spelt, emmer, barley, hemp and flax. We have also made, by double-digging and deep manuring, a vegetable plot to demonstrate generally rather than genetically that early medieval monastic and domestic gardens alike would have grown peas, beans and something like our unimproved Tynemouth cabbage, produced from seeds collected from the cliffs below Tynemouth monastery.

In 1995, while our first aim was, as previously, to demonstrate to visitors a range of arable crops available for growing on St Paul's seventh-century monastic estate, the first serious mini-experiment was conducted. It is of the simplest, counting grains sown, in drills and broadcast, and then counting the grain produced; of no great moment, but the beginning of a long haul to build up a databank of what can happen in these environmental circumstances using different methods. We have also begun trials, arising from hints in archaeological and documentary evidence, with different types of spade and hoe, of ard, plough and traction. Two mobile manuring machines, otherwise called Dexter cattle, occasionally provide unwilling traction or haulk a sullen log; but we have a very long way to go indeed before we can begin to emulate the lifetime of exemplary work in this field now laid before us from Denmark (Lerche 1994). We are also building. A multi-million pound new museum building reflects the inspiration of Mediterranean early Christian architecture to Evans and Shalev in the 1990s just as it did, according to Bede, to Benedict Biscop in the 670s. Our Anglian hall is based on the ground plan of Thirlings A, the *grubenhauser* on an excavated example from Hartlepool. Both are being constructed as experimental models, not just to see what they look like but to find out how such things might have been built and with what materials acquired from where. Once we have learnt about such matters, and have mastered the necessary crafts, we plan to build King Edwin's palace at Yeavering. Its ground plan lies already marked out in the grass at *Gywre* and a daunting site it is. Extrapolating from our experience with Thirlings A so far, a structure sponsored by Northern Rock Building Society, King Edwin would have needed a mortgage of the order of at least £150,000 at 1995 prices to erect a hall appropriate for a regnal sparrow to fly in one end and out the other. Still, that's life, as Bede would doubtless have noted down.

As much as anything, Bede's World is a medium of communication about the early medieval world to the present day. The workings of farming in an agrarian society – indeed the very nature of an agrarian society, so alien in the post-industrial context of South Tyneside – are an integral part of that message. We have not added anything yet to scientific knowledge of early medieval farming, but we have already learnt a lot ourselves and can increasingly share the learning and the experience with others. In an age when, sadly, many find themselves with too much time on their hands, there may be merit in extending some people's time horizon from merely the immediate present to thirteen centuries. Perhaps even more important in the long run may be an institution based on the idea of learning, a respect for the written word and the transmission of culture through scholarship and personal commitment to a vision.

Souped-up museums and virtual heritage may well have their place in the future presentation of the past but there still seems some merit, for research, interpretative and personal reasons, in making a landscape in the image of our best understanding of these things. The Anglian landscape of Bede's World may turn out some time in the future to be an unintentional landscape monument, perhaps to our folly but in any case to our state of mind in the 1990s. But then, does not that exactly exemplify what we believe all our landscapes to be about? – 'a trifle historical'. I think Christopher Taylor would buy that one, even if it is Northumbrian!

Bibliography

Archaeological Services, 1996, *The Ingram and Upper Breamish Valley Landscape Project. Interim Report 1996*. Durham and Morpeth. University of Durham and Northumberland National Park

Atkinson, F, 1977, *Life and Tradition in Northumberland and Durham*. London. Dent

Beckensall, S, 1983, *Northumberland's Prehistoric Rock Carvings. A Myth Explained*. Rothbury. Pendulum Publications

Beckensall, S, 1992, *Northumberland Place-Names*. Rothbury. Butler Publishing

Boniface, P, and Fowler, P, 1989, *Northumberland and Newcastle upon Tyne*. Aylesbury. Shire

Burgess, C B, 1968, *Bronze Age Metalwork in Northern England c.1000–700 BC*. Newcastle upon Tyne. Museum of Antiquities, Newcastle upon Tyne

Chapman, J C, and Mytum, H C, (eds), 1983, *Settlement in North Britain, 1000 BC – AD 1000* (= BAR British Series 118). Oxford. British Archaeological Reports

Clack, P, and Gosling, P, 1976, *Archaeology in the North*. Durham. Northern Archaeological Survey

Eagles, J, 1991, *Landscape and Community: A World Heritage Site in Rural Northumberland*. (Unpublished M.Litt. Thesis, Department of Archaeology, University of Newcastle upon Tyne)

Fowler, P J, 1986–8, Fieldwork in Northumberland. *Archaeological Reports from the Universities of Durham and Newcastle upon Tyne*, 1986, 9–11; 1987, 10–12; 1988, 3–4

Fowler, P J, 1989, English uplands, south-west and north-east: Local history and archaeology at inter-regional level. In R Higham (ed), *Landscape and Townscape in the South West* (= Exeter Studies in History 22). Exeter. University of Exeter. 1–17

Fowler, P J, 1992, A chapel and its context: Ebb's Nook, Beadnell, Northumberland. *Archaeology North*, 4, 9–13

Fowler, P J, 1993, Ebb's Nook, Beadnell, Northumberland. *Archaeological Reports from the Universities of Durham and Newcastle upon Tyne*, 1993, 45–50

Fowler, P J, 1995, Writing on the countryside. In I Hodder, M Shanks, A Alexandré, V Buchli, J Carman, J Last and G Lucas (eds), *Interpreting Archaeology. Finding Meaning in the Past.* London. Routledge. 100–109

Frazer, C, and Emsley, K, 1989, *Northumbria*. Chichester. Phillimore

Gibson, A M, 1978, *Bronze Age Pottery in the North-East of England* (= BAR British Series 56). Oxford. British Archaeological Reports

Grundy, J, 1992, *The Buildings of England: Northumberland*. Harmondsworth. Penguin

Harding, A F, 1981, Excavations in the prehistoric ritual complex near Milfield, Northumberland. *Proceedings of the Prehistoric Society*, 47, 87–135

Higham, N, 1986, *A Regional History of England. The Northern Counties to AD 1000*. London. Longman

House, J W, 1969, *Industrial Britain: The North East*. Newton Abbot. David and Charles

Johnson, N, and Rose, P, 1994, *Bodmin Moor. An Archaeological Survey. Volume 1: The Human Landscape to c1800* (Historic Buildings and Monuments Commission for England Archaeological Report 24 / RCHME Supplementary Series 11). London. Cornwall Archaeological Unit; Historic Buildings and Monuments Commission for England; Royal Commission on the Historical Monuments of England

Lerche, G, 1994, *Ploughing Implements and Tillage Practices in Denmark from the Viking Period to about 1800 Experimentally Substantiated*. Herning. Poul Kristensen

McCord, N, 1991, *North-East History from the Air*. Chichester. Philimore

Mercer, R, and Tipping, R, 1994, The prehistory of soil erosion in the northern and eastern Cheviot Hills, Anglo-Scottish Borders. In S Foster and T C Smout (eds), *The History of Soils and Field Systems*. Aberdeen. Scottish Cultural Press. 1–25

Miket, R, 1976, The evidence for Neolithic activity in the Milfield Basin, Northumberland. In C Burgess and R Miket (eds), *Settlement and Economy in the Third and Second Millennia BC* (= BAR British Series 33). Oxford. British Archaeological Reports. 113–42

Miket, R, 1981, Pit alignments in the Milfield Basin and the excavation of Ewart 1. *Proceedings of the Prehistoric Society*, 47, 137–46

Miket, R, and Burgess, C, (eds), 1984, *Between and Beyond the Walls. Essays on the Prehistory and History of North Britain in Honour of George Jobey*. Edinburgh. John Donald

Morley, D, and Robins, K, 1995, *Spaces of Identity. Global Media, Electronic Landscapes and Cultural Boundaries*. London. Routledge

Morris, C D, 1977, Northumbria and the Viking settlement: The evidence for land-holding. *Archaeologia Aeliana* (series 5), 5, 81–104

Musgrove, F, 1990, *The North of England. A History from Roman Times to the Present*. Oxford. Blackwell

Newton, R, 1972, *The Northumberland Landscape*. London. Hodder and Stoughton

Reynolds, P J, 1979, *Iron Age Farm: The Butser Experiment*. London. British Museum Publications

RCHM, 1990 *An Architectural Survey of Urban Development Corporation Areas: Tyne and Wear Volume One: Tyneside*. London. Royal Commission on the Historical Monuments of England

Sharp, T, 1937, *Northumberland. A Shell Guide*. London. Faber and Faber

Stancliff, C, and Cambridge, E, (eds), 1995, *Oswald: Northumbrian King to European Saint*. Satmford. P Watkins

Tait, J, 1965, *Beakers from Northumberland*. Newcastle upon Tyne. Museum of Antiquities, Newcastle upon Tyne

Taylor, C, 1970, *Dorset*. London. Hodder and Stoughton

Taylor, C, 1973, *The Cambridgeshire Landscape*. London. Hodder and Stoughton

Tegner, H, 1970, *Charm of the Cheviots*. Newcastle upon Tyne. Frank Graham

Tomlinson, W W, 1888, *Comprehensive Guide to Northumberland*. (reprinted 1985, Newcastle upon Tyne, Davies Books)

Topping, P, 1989, Early cultivation in Northumberland and the Borders. *Proceedings of the Prehistoric Society*, 55, 161–79

Turner, J, 1983, Some pollen evidence for the environment of north Britain 1000 BC to AD 1000. In J C Chapman and H C Mytum (eds), *Settlement in North Britain, 1000 BC – AD 1000* (= BAR British Series 118). Oxford. British Archaeological Reports. 3–28

van der Veen, M, 1992, *Crop Husbandry Regimes: An Archaeobotanical Study of Farming in Northern England 1000 BC – AD 500* (= Sheffield Archaeological Monographs 3). Sheffield. J R Collis Publications, University of Sheffield.

Waddington, C, 1977, *Land of Legend. Discovering the Heart of Ancient North Northumberland*. Milfield. The Country Store

6   Landscapes and the archaeologist

Timothy Darvill

Introduction

Twenty-five years is an exceedingly short time in the history of the English landscape, but a very long time in the development of studies connected with the archaeology of the landscape. In 1970, when Christopher Taylor first published his book on Dorset (Taylor 1970), the notion that landscape could be a major field of archaeological research was not at all common. Sites and monuments were the currency in which archaeologists traded, a fact underlined by the birth of the first county Sites and Monuments Records at about the same time (Benson 1972).

While Taylor's book on Dorset was not the first regional study to deal with archaeological aspects of the landscape, its appearance coincided with connections being made between geography, archaeology and the opening-up of the field of landscape studies for the archaeologist (Aston and Rowley 1974, 12). Papers published in the journal *Antiquity* illustrate the trend: in 1970, 1.6 per cent of the papers printed in the four issues for that year dealt with some aspect of landscape archaeology; in 1994–5, 11.5 per cent of papers dealt with this theme.[1] The increased interest by archaeologists in landscape since 1970 has been tremendous, and so too changes in the appreciation, understanding and approach to the idea of landscape.

Interestingly, the county of Dorset has unwittingly played a leading role in these changes through being host to a number of internationally significant projects that, little by little, have helped move forward the study of ancient landscapes. The archaeology of Dorset is so rich, and the projects so numerous, that it is difficult to select the most important. A few examples drawn from the field of prehistoric studies illustrate something of the overall contribution: Roger Mercer's work centred on Hambledon Hill in the north-west of the county (Mercer 1980); the investigations in Cranborne Chase by Martin Green which have prompted a number of papers on landscape change (Barratt *et al.* 1991; Tilley 1994); Collin Bowen's study of Bockerley Dyke in the east of the county (Bowen 1990); the excavations and fieldwork within and around Maiden Castle by English Heritage (Sharples 1991); Peter Woodward's survey of the South Dorset Ridgeway (Woodward 1991); and Barry Cunliffe's work on the coast at Hengistbury Head (Cunliffe 1987). No doubt similar lists could be drawn up with reference to Romano-British and later periods.

Celebrating the 25th anniversary of the publication of *Dorset* in *The Making of the English Landscape* series provides an opportunity to review changing perspectives from the benchmark offered by such a seminal work, while also looking forward towards some of the new directions offered by more recent work. In this short paper I would like to address just three issues. First, to look briefly at the way archaeological interest in the idea of landscape has developed; second to review critically some of the approaches used in archaeological work in the light of recent studies and researches in related disciplines; and, third, to examine a number of spheres in which archaeology enhances the contemporary experience of landscape while providing insights into its past. Before embarking on this, however, the very term 'landscape', which pervades this paper, needs some consideration and explanation.

Landscape

Recently, the term 'landscape' has been highjacked and perverted so often it has now become seriously devalued in intellectual terms. To many it has become a synonym for the countryside in general, to others it is a trendy-sounding cover-term for what might more properly be called a settlement pattern. The idea of a 'political landscape' has found currency in some quarters, and Robert Sandall, writing in *The Sunday Times*, has extended application still further into the realm of the conceptual, suggesting that 'the pop landscape now looks like a rather lumpy mix of ancient monuments and bright young things' (Sandall 1995).

The origins of the word landscape have been explored by a number of writers (Cosgrove 1985; Jackson 1986; Coones 1992, 23) who all trace it back to an Anglo-Saxon usage corresponding to the German word *landschaft* meaning a sheaf, a small-scale patch of cultivated land, but note that such a usage had gone out of vogue by the eleventh century. The term 'landscape' was re-coined in the seventeenth century, tied closely to the idea of a particular way of seeing things – specialized experiences of time and place – introduced into English from the Dutch *landskap* with explicit reference to visual expression through pictorial art (and see Howard 1991, 1).

But there is more to this issue of definition and meaning than mere semantics. The concept expressed by the term landscape is an important and interesting one which is relevant to many fields of inquiry. As Bender has argued (1993, 1), the idea of landscape in its broad sense should not be restrictively applied to the emergent capitalist world of early post-medieval western Europe which found the need to revive the term. As a concept linked very closely to experience and engagement, it embraces much more widely applicable themes about the relationship between people, the realm of ideas and values, and the world which they have created for themselves to live in.

From the archaeological perspective, an approach to landscape based on perception, and grounded in social context, is especially important because of the opportunities it opens up for the exploration of ancient landscapes. This is a matter that I will return to later, but before investigating such ideas further it is appropriate to develop an understanding of where we are now.

Landscapes in archaeology

Pinpointing the moment when archaeologists first became interested in the idea of landscape is impossible because so much depends on the way approaches and ideas are defined. During the inter-war period Carl Sauer was among the first geographers to express the view that, under the influence of a given culture the landscape became the repository of that culture's strivings against its environment and the tangible record of man's adaptation to the physical milieu. In this, culture was the agent, the natural environment the medium, and the cultural landscape the result (Sauer 1925; Gold 1980, 34). In Britain, the application of geographical models and principles to an understanding of the past can be traced back to the works of Cyril Fox (1933) and O G S Crawford (1953), among others, while the aesthetic value of landscape in an archaeological context is well exemplified in the works of Heywood Sumner (1913; 1917) working in Dorset and Hampshire, and E J Burrow (1919; 1924) in Somerset and Gloucestershire.

Studies by Maurice Beresford (1954; 1957), again drawing on ideas from historical geography, provide an important landmark in the investigation of medieval settlements and landscape. More or less coincident with much of Beresford's work was the publication in 1955 of W G Hoskins' book *The Making of the English Landscape*. This volume inspired many young archaeologists to translate the evolutionary perspective of their own discipline to the task of unravelling the complexities of the countryside.

In many ways, the publication of Hoskins' book laid the foundations for what is today called 'landscape archaeology' and which, since the early 1960s, has developed in leaps and bounds through a series of changing orientations, expanding methodologies (Aston and Rowley 1974), and links with landscape history. Initially, interest was grounded in the topographic analysis of landscape, the relationships between individual sites and between sites and their position in the countryside or townscape. Later, the positivist traditions of archaeological theory redirected interest towards the macro-region and the environmental setting of sites. The view that sites were nodes in a system which could be likened to a network took hold, and morphogenic studies which traced trajectories of change within such networks became common. In this view, well illustrated by numerous papers in the volume *Man, settlement and urbanism* (Ucko *et al.* 1972) landscape was often taken as a frame within which to view cultural history; a constraining factor on social and economic organization and on settlement patterns. Yet again, geography provided models and paradigms which archaeologists happily used (Clarke 1972; 1977; Hodder and Orton 1976, 53–97).

More recently, social archaeology has contributed to the examination of landscapes with an emphasis on the community and attention to linkages between people and their achievements (e.g. Bender 1993; Bradley 1993).

Within this kaleidoscope of changing theoretical orientations, it is possible to glimpse the application of many complementary approaches to the analysis of landscape: for example what has been called 'total archaeology' (Taylor 1974), historic landscape studies, site catchment analysis, environmental reconstruction and so on (Darvill 1992). In most of the studies carried out over the last 30 years or so, the landscape has been viewed by archaeologists in one of two distinct ways: as an object or as a subject.

Landscape as 'object'

Over the last three decades archaeologists have frequently viewed the landscape as a physical phenomenon which is essentially a human construction: an object or artefact that could be measured, quantified and understood in functionalist terms just like a ceramic vessel or a flint axe. Counting the number of sites in an area, relating them to each other and relating them to the terrain in which they lie has become an increasingly sophisticated task, often involving the use of many different strands of evidence: for example, cropmarks on aerial photographs, earthworks mapped by field survey, depictions on ancient maps and the texts of historic documents. The more techniques that can be brought to bear, the more detail can be discovered.

Understanding the landscape as an artefact has mainly involved looking at man-land relationships in locational or economic terms, emphasizing the way in which people have individually or collectively moulded and shaped the physical appearance of the landscape and, conversely, the ways in which the landscape has affected human activities.

The proceedings of the two conferences on the effect of man on the landscape, organized by the Council for British Archaeology in 1974 and 1975 (Evans *et al*. 1975; Limbrey and Evans 1978), illustrate very well this view of landscape as artefact, and connect it back to the work of Cyril Fox whose book *The Personality of Britain* was first published in 1932 and so eloquently expounds the ways in which the physical geography of the British Isles influenced early populations. The idea of ancient people 'making' the landscape is axiomatic to Hoskins' thesis, finding expression not only in the title of his book, but also in the text:

> What I have done is to take the landscape of England as it appears today, and to explain as far as I am able how it came to assume its present form, how the details came to be inserted, and when. (Hoskins 1955, 15)

More than anything else, treating the landscape as an object has drawn attention to just how much archaeology there is in the countryside. Historic features seem to be scattered everywhere and, typically, those places where they are most visible have often been termed 'historic landscapes' by land managers and conservationists because they combine the ancient and the modern in a rather special way (Swanwick 1982). In those places where archaeological remains are especially abundant, and where a good deal of what was created in the past survives, opportunities for a second approach to the archaeology of landscape presents itself: landscape as subject.

Landscape as 'subject'

Treating landscapes as subjects involves reconstructing earlier states of existence by, in effect, turning the clock back to create an image of a landscape as it might have been at some defined stage in its past. The descriptive technologies of mapping and reconstruction drawing provide familiar devices to communicate these ideas as they are used widely by later twentieth-century western societies to access modern landscapes. By selectively excluding earlier and later elements of the archaeological record a sort of quasi-historical map of an area can be built up to show the disposition of sites and monuments as they might have been arranged at a particular time. Success in this generally depends on having enough recorded elements or components to fit together into a pattern: such patterns are generally regarded as self-defining in the sense that they make themselves through the spatial juxtaposition and stratigraphic interconnection of components.

These approaches have also been carried over into the field of environmental reconstruction. In this sphere, attempts have been made, often quite successfully, to chart the way a piece of countryside has evolved in terms of its changing vegetation, soil cover, fauna and climate. Again, these things can be reconstructed and communicated through mapping and depiction.

The physical manifestation of landscapes rich in archaeology, and well researched in terms of their environment, means that now and again the past can almost be conjured up from the ground and brought to life: this amounts to what is sometimes called the 'historic environment'. In such places, it is argued, one is momentarily taken back into history: imagining what it was like in the eighteenth century when a magnificent ornamental park was set out, or standing in a village flanked by an open field system in the eleventh century AD or roaming among the freshly constructed mounds of a Bronze Age barrow cemetery.

But of course, these images and feelings are nothing to do with the Bronze Age or the medieval period, or the 18th century: what is being experienced is in the present and is based upon a perceptual framework that is entirely the product of our own socialization and background.

Critique of archaeological approaches to landscape

Treating landscapes either as objects or as subjects for reconstruction have been important stages in the development of thinking about archaeological approaches to landscape, but neither does justice to what, if examined closely, the idea of landscape is really about. Five particular problems can be identified.

First is the continued emphasis on defined sites and monuments. Many landscape studies in archaeology take the form of inventories: lists, maps and plans of individual monuments. This is done despite the fact that a broad understanding of the idea of social space is well established in archaeological thinking at several different scales. It is widely recognized that the environment or lifespace which is relevant to any community is much bigger and more extensive than the sort of loci that are most clearly visible archaeologically. People did not only exist within the confines of definable sites and monuments, they occupied territories and regions which had integrity, structure and symbolic meaning. Archaeological interest focuses not just on what happens within sites but also what is going on, in social terms, at spatial scales well above that. A distinction needs to be drawn, as Yi-Fu Tuan has done (1977), between 'place' as something nodal and closely defined, and 'space' as a more abstract framework, parts of which can be valued differentially by those who experience it.

Second is the idea that archaeological remains will be everywhere in the landscape. The elements which articulate spatial and stratigraphic relationships between areas of dense archaeology may sometimes be extremely subtle; natural features such as rivers and lakes and even apparently empty spaces may be as important in the context of landscape as barrows, tracks or any other visible and familiar man-made feature. As papers in the volume edited by

Carmichael and others (1994) amply show, apparently empty spaces can be 'constructed' and categorized and can, in social terms, sometimes be the most significant. Similarly, the massive distinctive natural granite tors of Bodmin Moor appear to have been a focus of interest in Mesolithic and later times (Tilley 1996; Darvill 1996, 170) even though their actual form was not changed. Strange rock formations, glacial erratics and erosion features in other parts of the country may also have been special places for early communities (see cover picture).

Third is the emphasis placed on the primacy of the physical dimensions of landscape, essentially those that can be appreciated visually. Stimuli from other senses, and the feelings that they generate, are also significant in experiencing landscape: smells, sounds, textures, tastes, atmosphere. Mental images and constructs are much more important than commonly realized. These may be generated through memories of actual experiences or through secondary perception and the transformation of received images (Schama 1995). Such mental constructs do not physically exist, and can never actually be found in reality quite as visualized in the mind, yet they constitute the images which serve to represent what has been or can be experienced.

The fourth area of concern is the lack of attention given to the social dimensions of landscape. Great attention is given to the products of actions, but rarely to the nature or basis of those actions. Landscapes, it can be argued, involve the application of value systems to the categorization, appreciation, negotiation and understanding of the spaces encountered by people as individuals, groups or whole communities. The point can best be illustrated with reference to what are sometimes called 'natural landscapes'. Logically, there can by definition be no such thing as a 'natural landscape'; the very concept of what is 'natural' in contradistinction to what is 'not natural' is a social category susceptible to redefinition at any time. Thus as soon as something is categorized as a natural landscape it ceases to be so (if it ever was in the sense of having an independent autonomous existence prior to being recognized) because it has at that moment been brought into the realm of the social.

Axiomatic to recognizing the socially constructed nature of landscape is the appreciation that different value systems may be applied sequentially or in parallel to the categorization, appreciation and renegotiation of any landscape. This is what gives landscapes a time-depth and means that they are regularly contested in terms of the value systems applying to them.

The final point to consider here is the matter of dynamics and the question of change. It is often assumed that the normal state for a landscape, as indeed for society generally, is a stable one which is more or less constant within certain bounds. This is a view born of the translation of systems theory and steady-state modelling from the field of electronics to the social sciences. It can be argued, however, that in fact the normal state for landscapes is one of constant change, and in particular change at many different levels and at many different rates. This is one reason why no two experiences of a landscape can ever be the same. Something will always be different: perhaps something as simple as the light or the weather, or perhaps a shift in value sets and the social categories applied to what is encountered. Here the balance between physical existence and social categories is particularly important because social constructs can effectively blind people to physical change that would be clear to an outsider. Thus a hillside which was once covered in woodland may continue to be treated, in social terms, as a wooded place even though the trees have gone. The old order will be perpetuated through such devices as myths, legends and place-names which stimulate memories and mental images at odds with what is observed.

Taking into account these difficulties with the archaeological treatment of landscapes it is pertinent to ask what alternative perspectives are available? In answering such a question it has to be admitted that a number of approaches are currently at what might be termed an experimental stage. Hermeneutics and time-space geography (Thomas 1993), politics and perception (Bender 1993), human eco-dynamics (McGlade 1995), and the differential social structuring of space (Parker Pearson and Richards 1994) represent some of the nodes around which thinking about landscape is currently developing. Elsewhere I have outlined an archaeologically relevant model of landscape based on the interpenetration of three themes – time, space and social action – based in large measure on sociological theory (Darvill 1994; 1997). At about the same time Christopher Tilley presented an interesting approach based on phenomenology which involves the understanding and description of things as they are experienced by individuals: the relationship between being and being-in-the-world (Tilley 1994, 12). Both models share a number of features, one of which is the recognition of what can be called 'social space'.

For archaeology, the starting point is the acceptance that in the past, as now, people live and work within a large space or environment within which they are free to move about according to socially-defined rules and expectations. Every piece of such a social space is identified with a series of attributed values and meanings as if the space itself is categorized or compartmentalized in the minds of its inhabitants even if not physically through boundaries and edges. Some categories superficially appear functional and straightforward: fields, pasture, house or burial ground. Others are more deeply embedded in human emotions and feelings: burial grounds that mix images of darkness and the spirits of the ancestors, woods that disorientate and confuse and springs that give new life and link the land of the living with the underworld.

The values or meanings attributed to different parts of the environment dictate the way that people relate to it, move about within it and what actually happens there. A rather topical modern example would be the special values placed on Britain's National Parks because of their perceived aesthetic beauty and their role in recreation, leisure, conservation and the heritage in its broadest sense (Edwards 1991). These spaces have effectively become sacred places for today's population and this finds expression in the material culture found in them and the consequent limitations on what it is acceptable to do there. Archaeological evidence is less easy to handle than contemporary observation and it is often impossible to understand the values that prehistoric people attributed to sectors of their landscape. However, anthropological studies of various kinds suggest a number of avenues of approach that may be relevant.

First, the categorization of space is generally systematic and the rules which inform the understanding of each category often relate to underlying beliefs and cosmologies. Tuan (1977, 34) has argued that because the human body has a distinct upright position the spaces that open out before an individual are immediately differentiable into front-back, left-right, up-down axes, and that these are frequently extrapolated onto an area in conformity with the

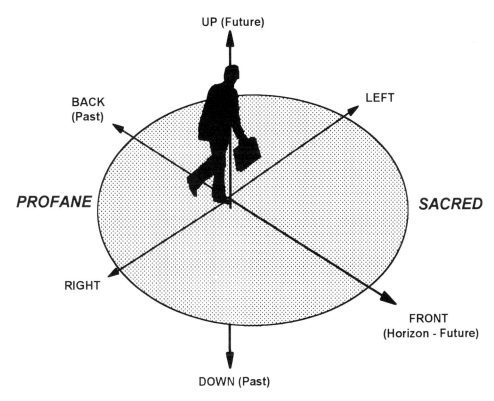

Fig. 6.1. Projection of space in relation to an upright human body [after Tuan 1977, fig. 2 with additions].

structure and position of the body itself (Figure 6.1). Sennett (1994) has taken this relationship between the human body and physical space still further by discussing the ways in which both the form of the human body, and social attitudes to it, have shaped the layout and structure of cities as rather special kinds of landscape in western civilizations since classical times.

Second, the categorization of space is often 'nested' in the sense that arrangements apply at several different levels simultaneously: for example within the home, in the layout of a settlement and in the environment as a whole. This means that if patterns can be detected strongly at one level they may be applicable at another. Numerous cases of such nesting can be identified, but one of the most fully documented is represented by the Pirá-Paraná Indians of Columbia studied by Christine Hugh-Jones (1979) who shows that daily life on all levels and at all scales is structured through a series of horizontal and vertical space-time models. Myths say that an ancestral anaconda snake come up the river from the east, stopping to create descent groups by giving birth to men by the side of the river. At its most simple, the river provides a linear order to everyday life while the environment itself provides a concentric order. Together these basic models provide a means of classifying space and action within a series of systems raging in scale from the earth as a whole, where houses can be built, what happens within the houses, the body and the womb. Oppositions are created by linking elements occupying similar places in the two orders across different systems. In this way, everything that these communities experience and do is linked together and given meaning within the structure of their belief system or cosmology.

A relationship between general belief systems and the ordering and structuring of space is surprisingly common. Wheatley (1977) provides a detailed analysis of the origins and character of ancient Chinese cities, recognizing the cosmological ordering of space. One example of this can be seen in the way the main processional axis of a city ran from north to south to reflect a celestial meridian. This meant that any roads on this alignment had greater significance than those running east to west. Similar, but more complex, sacred geographies have been explored by Richer (1994) in relation to the architecture and landscapes of ancient Greek states. Here, astral schemes are translated from the heavens to structure and lend symbolic meaning to the arrangement of space.

A third general proposition relating to the relationship between space and landscape is that the organization of space finds expression in the patterning of material culture. Just as within a house the walls, furniture, doors, windows and the use of light and shade dictate the way people move around within the structure, react to it and to one another and do certain things in certain places (Parker Pearson and Richards 1994), so it is with the wider landscape. The things in the landscape are the material reflections of the way it is used. Fences, boundaries, gates, tracks, stones, monuments, structures, views and vistas are among the devices commonly used to make the landscape work and have meaning. Thus the landscape is not a passive thing – the product of everything that has gone on before – but an active thing, the very matrix in which social life is conducted.

Landscapes are dynamic because values and meanings are constantly redefined and renegotiated. Areas at one time highly valued become of lesser value later. Thus in some periods hilltop positioning was a very significant factor in the location of settlements, at other times the only places not used for settlements were hilltops. How people in any society choose to use the space in which they find themselves is entirely a social phenomenon. Part of the process of choosing and valuing places is the extent to which the material culture of past arrangements is selectively retained or destroyed, consciously or unconsciously, during the creation of the new devices relevant to the prosecution of action with revised values and meanings.

Archaeology in landscapes

Having some theoretical handles on the matter of archaeology and landscape is one thing, but making use of them is quite another. In recent years, archaeological perspectives have contributed a great deal to contemporary studies of landscape in several ways. In this final section I would like to touch on three rather critical levels of understanding which are relevant to the future of landscape archaeology not only as an academic pursuit but also as a contributor to landscape management in general and archaeological resource management in particular.

Archaeology all around

It is now widely recognized that the modern contemporary landscape contains an abundance of archaeological remains of many different dates and purposes. Most such remains, especially the older ones, have long ago become isolated sites and monuments without the context they once had within a wider system. All, however, contribute to understanding the evolution of the spaces they occupy, and in some cases continue to influence contemporary action and give texture and character to the modern landscape. Drawing on some of the concepts explained above, the reasons for this are clear. Today's landscape is a web of differently-valued spaces created and maintained by different individuals and groups for a variety of reasons. The survival of archaeological remains is contingent on the socially-defined values assigned to those spaces. Thus every time a road is diverted or a development proposal quashed in order to avoid an archaeological site, bits of our contemporary landscape are revalued in favour of a past that may not, in all honesty, be very well understood. When the reverse happens, and archaeological remains are destroyed, other values have been attached to the spaces concerned.

Assigning values to the spaces which represent our contemporary landscape has become both difficult and controversial (Countryside Commission 1996). Many different pressures impinge on the way space is used, while the variety of reasons why specific areas might be considered important seems to grow daily. In response, the process of landscape assessment has developed as a technique that provides a structured approach to the reconciliation of conflicts between interests at a relatively localized scale (Countryside Commission 1991; 1993; and see Herring and Johnson, this volume). This is achieved through three successive stages: description, classification and evaluation. Archaeology is one of the many factors commonly considered by landscape assessment programmes, although there are no accepted methods for measuring the 'archaeologicalness' of a given area. However, what landscape assessment cannot do is replace the ultimate need to assign socially-defined values to things and arrangements.

At a broader scale mapping landscape character can help clarify the contributions made by different elements, both historical and contemporary, and highlight what makes an area what it is today. A number of such maps are currently in preparation at regional and national level (Countryside Commission and English Nature 1996; and see Herring and Johnson, this volume), and, as for landscape assessment procedures, experiments are under way to find appropriate techniques for condensing the archaeological information into usable formats while retaining the integrity of the data itself.

Relict cultural landscapes

Some sections of the modern landscape contain so much broadly contemporary archaeology that their current arrangement closely resembles that created when they were last systematically restructured: they represent relics of the pattern of material culture resulting from the value systems of some previous age. In some cases they still structure behaviour to a greater or lesser extent, even though their original meanings have been lost. Such landscapes are well represented in south-western England as recent surveys of Cranborne Chase (RCHME 1975), Dartmoor (Fleming 1978; 1983) and Bodmin Moor (Johnson and Rose 1994) amply demonstrate.

From an archaeological point of view, these sites are extremely important because of they contain so many relationships and articulations between components. They are critical for understanding how specific places (here linked to the concept of sites) tie into the bigger spaces in which they lay (Darvill *et al*. 1993).

Relict cultural landscapes provide obvious blocks for the archaeologist to get to grips with in order to preserve elements of the archaeological record as a databank on our collective history. But the protection and conservation of such areas is proving to be something of a challenge. Approaches are being developed (Lambrick 1992), and the inclusion of archaeo-logically-rich areas within broader landscape assessments and mapping programmes will no doubt help in the long term.

But some caution must be applied. Set against their obvious appeal and great interest must be the fact that relict cultural landscapes survive only as islands within our own contempor-ary landscapes. They are only fragments of landscapes which were once much larger. Moreover, they have lost their original social context through being transformed into the modern contemporary landscape and thus lack the coherence and meaning that they once had: they are anachronisms within the modern countryside.

Ancient landscapes

The third aspect of landscape that is of interest to archaeology takes us beyond the relict cultural landscape to what I will call the ancient landscape, that is the pattern of spaces created and inhabited by earlier communities. It can be argued that if today's landscape has a basis in reality, then it is axiomatic that earlier communities occupying the same spaces also had a 'landscape' represented by their own idiosyncratic perception of space. As already indicated, there is good support for such a uniformitarian proposition from anthropological studies. From an academic standpoint, understanding the form and structure of an ancient landscape is critically important for understanding everything else about a time and place.

Our ability to comprehend ancient landscapes hinges on there being a relationship between the conceptualization of space, the representation of place and the nature and distribution of material culture. In this, social context becomes critically important, and again the link is well attested from anthropological and historical studies.

The biggest problem with ancient landscapes is one of data recovery. While relict cultural landscapes are often self-defining because of the relationship between the relict components and more recent changes, ancient landscapes are unlikely to be represented intact within the modern landscape simply because of their socially-defined character, large scale, and the erosive effects of landscape change. Thus the quest for ancient landscapes becomes an extensive and intensive piece of research on a scale that has hardly yet been attempted. And, whereas a bottom-up approach led by the survival of archaeological remains is a pragmatic solution to the definition of scattered sites and relict cultural landscapes, the identification of ancient landscapes needs a top-down approach in order to overcome the problems of scale, structure and attributed meaning (Darvill *et al*. 1993). In practice, this means having some understanding of the structuring principles that underlay the way the landscape was perceived and experienced.

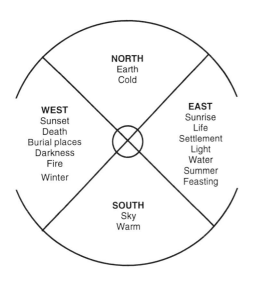

NORTH
Earth
Cold

WEST
Sunset
Death
Burial places
Darkness
Fire
Winter

EAST
Sunrise
Life
Settlement
Light
Water
Summer
Feasting

SOUTH
Sky
Warm

Fig. 6.2. Putative late Neolithic cosmology.

Tilley (1994) has recently considered the case of the later Neolithic landscape of Cranborne Chase, expanding on the earlier work of Barrett, Bradley and Green (1993). In both studies attention is drawn to the positioning of monuments to facilitate, prevent, structure and direct movements within the landscape. Space is seen as either distinctively sacred or profane, some of the movements within it being linked perhaps to the occurrence of significating solar events.

A close association between the orientation of many later Neolithic monuments and key solar events, for example the midsummer and midwinter sunrises, provide hints as to a possible cosmology for the period. Such a scheme can, very tentatively, be further developed into a four-fold horizontal subdivision of space (perhaps with vertical separation too) taking into account homologies between the structuring of space within the late Neolithic houses, tombs and henges of northern Scotland (Parker Pearson and Richards 1993, 41–7; Richards 1996). From these regularities it is possible to propose a series of provisional binary oppositions, specifically linked to body structures and, through the solar cosmology, to specific axes and alignments (Figure 6.2). Central to the cosmology is the sun as a transforming phenomenon: darkness into light, cold into warmth, summer into winter and so on. In some cases the sun may be represented by a hearth set in the centre of a defined space.

Applying the model is not made easy by the need to define the pivotal point in the scheme. One area where it can be seen to work well is around Stonehenge where the orientation of the monument and its avenue gives a very clear axis to the local structuring of space (Darvill 1997). Something similar may be visible in Dorset at the well-known concentration of later Neolithic monuments around Dorchester, Dorset.

The archaeology of a late Neolithic landscape:
The Dorchester Area, Dorset

Researches over the last 20 years, prompted in large measure by development pressure, has led to the discovery and excavation of over a dozen major sites dating to the period around 2500 BC. Most lie on the interfluve between the River Frome and the River South Winterbourne, although the surrounding uplands and river valleys themselves are also important. Undoubtedly there is more to find, but what is available already gives a clear glimpse of an ancient landscape (for general summaries see RCHME 1970; Lawson 1990; Sharples 1991; Woodward 1991).

Pursuing the idea that the structuring of space should be recognizable in the patterning of material culture at a number of different levels, it is pertinent to start with a relatively small scale. The henge-enclosure of Mount Pleasant, excavated in 1970–1 by Geoffrey Wainwright, provides one such place (Wainwright 1979). Here, inside the henge-enclosure on the highest part of the site, is a classic class I henge monument (Site IV). It comprises an enclosed space some 43m in diameter defined by a ditch, 3m-4m wide and up to 2m deep, with an external bank. The interior was accessible via a single entrance through the boundary earthwork, 7.5m wide, opening to the north-east. In the interior was a timber structure represented by five concentric rings of postholes with a maximum diameter of 38.0m. Radiocarbon dates show that the structure was constructed about 2561–2457 BC (average of BM-663, BM-666 and BM-667 from the primary phase of the structure); the associated material culture is dominated by Grooved Ware pottery.

The timber structure at Mount Pleasant Site IV is rather irregular in its construction, but is clearly designed around four corridors which divide the rings into quadrants. This, it can be argued, perpetuates in architectural form the four-fold division of space implicit in the provisional symbolic cosmology for the period (Figure 6.3). The main axis of the building is slightly to the north of north-east being aligned on the entrance through the surrounding earthwork and roughly on the midsummer sunrise. Finds from within the ditch of Site IV suggest that rubbish disposal focused on the north-west terminal of the enclosure ditch: perhaps an association with the earth. It is not clear what lay at the centre of the site contemporary with the timber structure, but during the re-modelling of Site IV in Phase II,

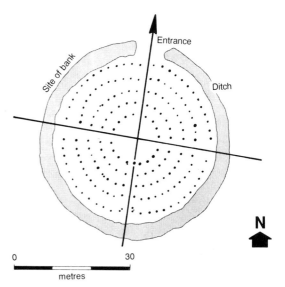

Fig. 6.3. Mount Pleasant Site IV, Dorchester, Dorset. Phase I [after Wainwright 1979, fig. 7].

the central area was occupied by a stone setting ('a cove'), square in plan, reminiscent of the central hearths in henges on Orkney (*cf.* Wainwright 1979, fig. 16 and Parker Pearson and Richards 1993, fig. 2.2).

Other monuments in the Dorchester area perpetuate a similar axis to that represented at Site IV (Figure 6.4). One is the Flagstones enclosure with its curious causewayed ditch which closely parallels Phase 1 at Stonehenge (Woodward 1988; Cleal *et al.* 1996, 63). The gap on the north-east side at Flagstones is marked by two small ditch segments evenly set within a much larger gap. Although only half the enclosure has been excavated, three out of the four human burials found in the primary ditch fills were situated in the western quadrant (Woodward 1988). A series of cremation burials set within a small ditched enclosure within

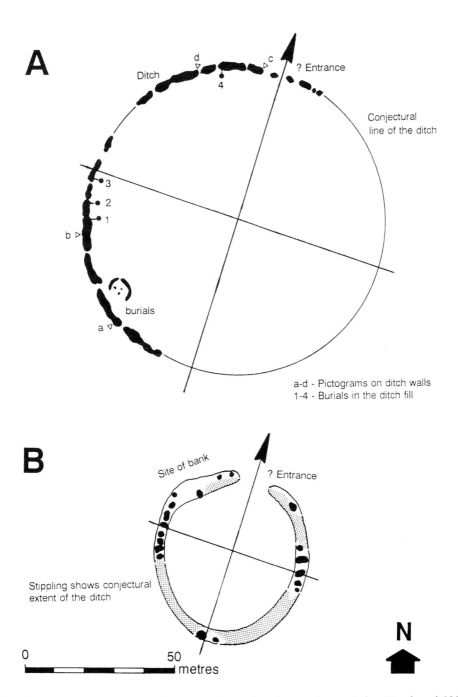

A

Ditch

? Entrance

Conjectural
line of the ditch

3

2

1

b

burials

a

a-d - Pictograms on ditch walls
1-4 - Burials in the ditch fill

B

Site of bank

? Entrance

Stippling shows conjectural
extent of the ditch

0   50
                    metres

N

Fig. 6.4. Flagstones enclosure and Maumbury Rings, Dorchester, Dorset [after Woodward 1988, fig. 2 and Bradley 1975, fig. 3].

the main enclosure also lay in this quadrant. The unique series of pictograms on the ditch walls were more evenly spread around the perimeter (Figure 6.4).

A north-eastern orientation is also represented at Maumbury Rings, in Roman times the site of an amphitheatre for the citizens of *Durnovaria*, but in the third millennium BC a class I henge monument (Bradley 1975). The henge is unusual in having a series of circular shafts extending up to 8m into the solid chalk from the bottom of the ditch. Insufficient of the site was examined to provide a full plan, but it is estimated that originally there were perhaps 45 shafts around the periphery, the central area being approximately 47m across. Although only eight of the shafts were fully explored, a total of 17 were examined in greater or lesser detail. Finds were generally rather scarce, but human bones were only found at depth in one shaft, number 10, on the west side of the monument. The elevated position of the site, its situation roughly half way between the River Frome and the South Winterbourne, and its nodal place in the middle of an extensive distribution of contemporary sites may be significant, and perhaps set it apart as a focal place.

At a larger scale, it is notable that outside both Mount Pleasant and Flagstones, on the west side, are late Neolithic burial monuments: the Conqueror Barrow at Mount Pleasant (Wainwright 1979, 65) and the Allington Avenue long mound and round barrows at Flagstones (Davies *et al.* 1985). The arrangement around Maumbury Rings is less clear because of the presence of modern settlement. However, excavations in 1988 and 1989 at Coburg Road revealed the presence of four substantial ring ditches, putatively of late Neolithic or early Bronze Age date, and perhaps representing the remains of a linear barrow cemetery extending along the ridge west of Maumbury (Smith *et al.* 1992).

In general then, it seems that both at the level of individual monuments, and within the immediate vicinity of these same site, there is some evidence for the formal structuration of space through regular patterning in layout and the disposition of material culture. The patterns seem to follow the provisional late-Neolithic cosmology discussed above. Can the same thing be seen at still wider scales?

Taking Maumbury Rings as a possible focal point in the landscape, and applying the same structuring principles as were used at a smaller scale for individual sites, an interesting regularity to the spaces within a putative territory centred on the Frome/South Winterbourne interfluve can be identified (Figure 6.5; and see Woodward 1990, fig. 68 on this and surrounding territorial units).

In the eastern quadrant (forward right if standing inside Maumbury Rings, *cf.* Figure 6.1 and Figure 6.5) are areas of settlement (including the henge-enclosure at Mount Pleasant) and the complex of ceremonial sites along Fordington Ridge between Mount Pleasant and Maumbury Rings. To the south are the two late-Neolithic pit circles on Conygar Hill (Woodward and Smith 1987, 84; Lawson 1990, 278–9), the eastern one associated with Peterborough pottery, the western one with Grooved Ware. There was no evidence for human burials associated with either structure, a common trait of such monuments which are usually seen as having a ceremonial function (Gibson 1994, 207).

In the western quadrant lie the majority of burial monuments, the long mound on Maiden Castle and an area believed to have been used for flintworking (Sharples 1990, fig. 28). The western limits of this quadrant are not well defined, and the abundance of late Neolithic

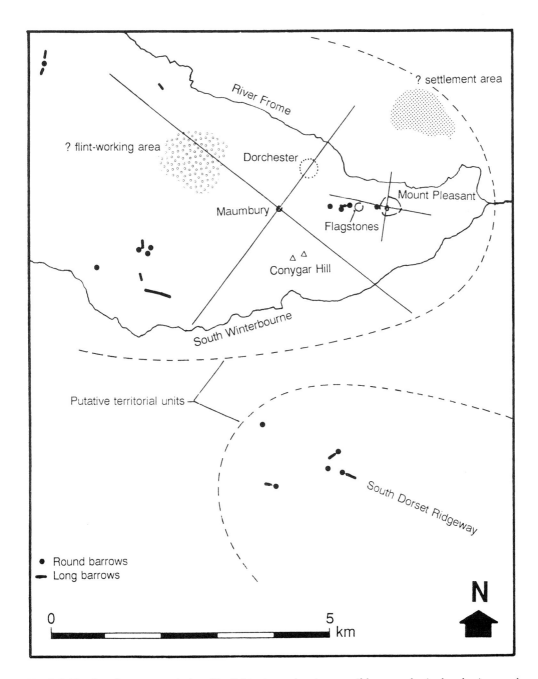

Fig. 6.5. The Dorchester area in late Neolithic times showing possible cosmological order imposed on the landscape [distributions based on Woodward 1991, fig. 68; Sharples 1991, fig. 28; and Lawson 1990, fig. 1].

ceremonial monuments extending westwards along the valley of the South Winterbourne hints that this zone may be very extensive.[2] In the northern quadrant is the large stockaded enclosure at Dorchester, built around 2700 BC, and perhaps straddling the main Maumbury axis (Woodward *et al.* 1984; Davies and Farwell 1989). Indeed, its similarity to other similar structures throughout the British Isles (Whittle 1991) suggests that perhaps it should be seen as the principal focus of this territory rather than Maumbury.

The whole arrangement of the Dorchester landscape is strikingly similar to that around Stonehenge, and of very similar scale (Darvill 1997). Not all the elements are clearly understood yet, but, at the very least, there appears to be some support for the investigation of the links between landscapes as socially-defined structures grounded in belief systems (cosmologies) and archaeological patterning.

Of course, it could be contended that the cosmological structure itself is poorly supported, and that in the absence of contemporary documentation for its basic form cannot be accepted. This is a reasonable argument, and in normal circumstances would have to be accepted at face value. Rather unusually for prehistoric times, however, there is some evidence which takes the basis for the partitioning of space by these communities as close to the people themselves as could be hoped for, and to a scale of application smaller even than that of a single site. At Flagstones, someone drew pictures on the wall of the enclosure ditch (Woodward 1988). One is particularly striking as it appears to show an elongated concentric arrangement with a marked axis represented by an opening in the central circuit (Figure 6.6A); interestingly, counting the central space and the space beyond the outer line, there are five zones: the same number as within the post-structure at Mount Pleasant.

But Flagstones is not the only clue. Also relevant is the fact that on the bottom of some beaker pots there is a cross-shaped pattern incised into the base of the vessel (Clarke 1970, 437). Perhaps most impressive of all are the small gold disks, so-called sun disks, from all over the British Isles which bear a central cross set within one or more concentric circles (Case 1977; Figure 6.6 B-D). Together, the commonality of design seen at the small-scale represented by decoration on single objects and at a large scale in the architectural design of particular monuments provides a powerful argument for the extension of similar structuring to the wider world in which the sites were set and the artifacts circulated.

Conclusion

In this short paper I have tried to show that over the past 25 years archaeologists have formed a close and firm link with the idea of landscape. Books such as that by Christopher Taylor which is celebrated in this volume form the foundation of that happy relationship. Looking forward, I am confident that landscape studies in archaeology will continue to grow for two main reasons. First, because of the increasing relevance of archaeological contributions to broader social debates about the future of the landscape and its management. And second, because of increasing insights and interest in the social archaeology of past societies in terms of their engagement with the world they created for themselves.

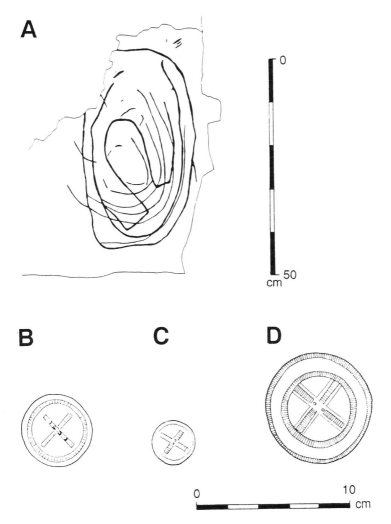

Fig. 6.6. Putative representations of late Neolithic cosmologies. A. Flagstones, Dorchester; B. Farleigh Wick, Wiltshire; C. Mere, Wiltshire; D. ?Ireland [A. after Woodward 1988, fig. 3a; B–D after Case 1977, fig. 2].

Notes

1 The four issues published in 1970 contained 61 papers and notes, of which 1 dealt with landscape. In the four issues published between March 1994 and March 1995 there were 68 papers and notes, of which 7 dealt with landscape.

2 A study of this area is currently (1997) being carried out by Mr Wayne Bennett, a postgraduate student in the School of Conservation Sciences, Bournemouth University

Timothy Darvill

Acknowledgements

A number of people provided comment and assistance in preparing this paper, and I would especially like to thank Dr John Coyne, Dr Jane Timby, Alex Hunt, Nicola King, Humphrey Case, Susan Davies, Ann Woodward and Peter Woodward for their helpful suggestions.

Bibliography

Aston, M, and Rowley, T, 1974, *Landscape Archaeology*. Newton Abbot. David and Charles

Barrett, J, Bradley, R, and Green, M, 1991, *Landscape, Monuments and Society: The Prehistory of Cranborne Chase*. Cambridge. Cambridge University Press

Bender, B, 1993, Introduction. Landscape: Meaning and action. In B Bender (ed), *Landscape: Politics and Perspectives*. Oxford. Berg. 1–18

Benson, D, 1973, A sites and monuments record for the Oxford region. *Oxoniensia*, 37, 226–237

Beresford, M W, 1954, *The Lost Villages of England*. London. Lutterworth

Beresford, M W, 1957, *History on the Ground*. London. Lutterworth

Bowen, H C, 1990, *The Archaeology of Bokerley Dyke*. London. Royal Commission on the Historical Monuments of England

Bradley, R, 1975, Maumbury Rings, Dorchester: The excavations of 1908–1913. *Archaeologia*, 105, 1–97

Bradley, R, 1993, *Altering the Earth* (= Society of Antiquaries of Scotland Monograph 8). Edinburgh. Society of Antiquaries of Scotland

Burrow, E J, 1919, *Ancient Entrenchments and Camps of Gloucestershire*. Cheltenham. E J Burrow and Co

Burrow, E J, 1924, *Ancient Earthworks and Camps of Somerset*. Cheltenham. E J Burrow and Co

Carmichael, D L, Hubert, J, Reeves, B, and Schanche, A, (eds), 1994, *Sacred Sites, Sacred Places* (= One World Archaeology 23). London. Routledge

Case, H, 1977, An early accession to the Ashmolean Museum. In V Markotic (ed), *Ancient Europe and the Mediterranean. Studies in Honour of Hugh Hencken*. Warminster. Aris and Phillips. 18–34

Clarke, D L, 1970, *Beaker Pottery of Great Britain and Ireland*. Cambridge. Cambridge University Press. (2 vols)

Clarke, D L, 1972, Models and paradigms in contemporary archaeology. In D L Clarke (ed), *Models in Archaeology*. London. Methuen. 1–60

Clarke, D L, (ed), 1977, *Spatial Archaeology*. London. Academic Press

Cleal, R M J, Walker, K E, and Montague, R, 1996, *Stonehenge in its Landscape. Twentieth-Century Excavations* (= English Heritage Archaeological Report 10). London. English Heritage

Coones, P, 1992, The unity of landscape. In L Macinnes and C R Wickham-Jones (eds) *All Natural Things. Archaeology and the Green Debate* (= Oxbow Monograph 21). Oxford. Oxbow Books. 22–40

Cosgrove, D, 1985, Prospect, perspective and the evolution of the landscape idea. *Transactions of the Institute of British Geographers*, (NS) 10, 45–62

Countryside Commission, 1991, *Assessment and Conservation of Landscape Character. The Warwickshire Landscape Project Approach* (= CCP 332). Cheltenham. Countryside Commission

Countryside Commission, 1993, *Landscape Assessment Guidance* (= CCP 423). Cheltenham. Countryside Commission

Countryside Commission, 1996, *Views from the Past.* (= CCWP 04). Cheltenham. Countryside Commission

Countryside Commission and English Nature, 1996, *The Character of England.* Cheltenham. Countryside Commission. (colour map and explanatory index)

Crawford, O G S, 1953, *Archaeology in the Field.* London. Phoenix

Cunliffe, B, 1987, *Hengistbury Head, Dorset. Volume 1: The Prehistoric and Roman Settlement 3500 BC – AD 500* (= OUCA Monograph 26). Oxford. Oxford University Committee for Archaeology

Darvill, T, 1992, *Monuments Protection Programme. Monument Evaluation Manual. Part III: Relict Cultural Landscapes.* London. English Heritage. [Circulated typescript report]

Darvill, T, 1994, *Neolithic Landscapes: Identity and Definition.* Paper presented to the Neolithic Studies Group Meeting held in the British Museum on 14th November 1994

Darvill, T, 1996, *Prehistoric Britain from the Air: A Study of Space, Time and Society.* Cambridge. Cambridge University Press

Darvill, T, 1997, Ever increasing circles: The sacred geographies of Stonehenge and its landscape. *Proceedings of the British Academy*, 92, 167–202

Darvill, T, Gerrard, C, and Startin, B, 1993, Identifying and protecting historic landscapes. *Antiquity*, 67, 563–74

Davies, S M, and Farwell, D, 1989, Charles Street, Dorchester, Wessex Court Development. *Proceedings of the Dorset Natural History and Archaeological Society*, 111, 107–9

Davies, S M, Stacey, L C, and Woodward, P J, 1985, Excavations at Allington Avenue, Fordington, Dorchester, 1984/5: Interim report. *Proceedings of the Dorset Natural History and Archaeological Society*, 107, 102–110

Edwards, R, 1991, *Fit for the Future. Report of the National Parks Review Panel* (= CCP 334). Cheltenham. Countryside Commission

Evans, J G, Limbrey, S, and Cleere, H, (eds), 1975, *The Effect of Man on the Landscape: The Highland Zone* (= CBA Research Report 11). London. Council for British Archaeology

Fleming, A, 1978, The prehistoric landscape of Dartmoor. Part 1. South Dartmoor. *Proceedings of the Prehistoric Society*, 44, 97–124

Fleming, A, 1983, The prehistoric landscape of Dartmoor part 2: North and east Dartmoor. *Proceedings of the Prehistoric Society*, 49, 195–242

Fox, C, 1933, *The Personality of Britain: Its Influence on Inhabitant and Invader in Prehistoric and Early Historic Times* (Second Edition). Cardiff. National Museum of Wales. (1st Edition 1932)

Gibson, A, 1994, Excavations at the Sarn-y-bryn-caled complex, Welshpool, Powys, and the timber circles of Great Britain and Ireland. *Proceedings of the Prehistoric Society*, 60, 143–223

Gold, J R, 1980, *An Introduction to Behavioural Geography.* Oxford. Oxford University Press

Grinsell, L V, 1959, *Dorset Barrows.* Dorchester. Dorset Natural History and Archaeological Society

Grinsell, L V, 1982, *Dorset Barrows: Supplement.* Dorchester. Dorset Natural History and Archaeological Society

Hodder, I, and Orton, C, 1976, *Spatial Analysis in Archaeology* (= New Studies in Archaeology 1). Cambridge. Cambridge University Press

Hoskins, W G, 1955, *The Making of the English Landscape.* London. Hodder and Stoughton

Howard, P, 1991, *Landscapes. The Artists' Vision.* London. Routledge

Hugh-Jones, C, 1979, *From the Milk River: Spatial and Temporal Processes in North-West Amazonia.* Cambridge. Cambridge University Press

Jackson, J B, 1986, The vernacular landscape. In E C Pennington-Rowsell and D Lowenthal (eds) *Landscape Meanings and Values.* London. Allen and Unwin. 65–81

Johnson, N, and Rose, P, 1994, *Bodmin Moor. An Archaeological Survey. Volume 1: The Human Landscape to c1800* (Historic Buildings and Monuments Commission for England Archaeological Report 24 / RCHME Supplementary Series 11). London. Cornwall Archaeological Unit; Historic Buildings and Monuments Commission for England; Royal Commission on the Historical Monuments of England

Lambrick, G, 1992, The importance of the cultural heritage in a green world: Towards the development of landscape integrity assessment. In L Macinnes and C R Wickham-Jones (eds) *All Natural Things. Archaeology and the Green Debate* (= Oxbow Monograph 21). Oxford. Oxbow Books. 105–126

Lawson, A, 1990, The prehistoric hinterland of Maiden Castle. *Antiquaries Journal*, 70, 271–287

Limbrey, S, and Evans, J G, (eds), 1978, *The Effect of Man on the Landscape: The Lowland Zone* (= CBA Research Report 21). London. Council for British Archaeology

McGlade, J, 1995, Archaeology and the ecodynamics of of human-modified landscapes. *Antiquity*, 69, 113–132

Mercer, R, 1980, *Hambledon Hill. A Neolithic Landscape*. Edinburgh. Edinburgh University Press

Parker Pearson, M, and Richards, C, 1994, Architecture and order: Spatial representation and archaeology. In M Parker Pearson, and C Richards (eds), *Architecture and Order. Approaches to Social Space*. London. Routledge. 38-72

RCHME, 1970, *An Inventory of Historical Monuments in the County of Dorset. Volume Two. South-East*. London. HMSO (3 parts)

RCHME, 1975, *An Inventory of Historical Monuments in the County of Dorset. Volume Five. East Dorset*. London. HMSO

Richards, C, 1996, Monuments as landscape: creating the centre of the world in late Neolithic Orkney. *World Archaeology*, 28.2, 190–208

Richer, J (translated by C Rhone), 1994, *Sacred geography of the Ancient Greeks: Astrological Symbolism in Art, Architecture and Landscape*. New York. State University of New York Press

Sandall, R, 1995, Don't rewind me. *The Sunday Times*, 29:1:1995, Part 10, 14

Sauer, C O, 1925, The morphology of landscape. Reprinted in J Leighley (ed), 1969, *Land and life: A Selection from the Writings of Carl Ortwin Sauer*. Berkeley. University of California Press. 315–350

Schama, S, 1995, *Landscape and Memory*. London. Harper-Collins

Sennett, R, 1994, *Flesh and Stone*. London. Faber and Faber

Sharples, N M, 1991, *Maiden Castle. Excavations and Field Survey 1985–6* (= Historic Buildings and Monuments Commission for England Archaeological Report 19). London. English Heritage

Smith, R J C, Rawlings, M N, and Barnes, I, 1992, Excavations of Coburg Road and Weymouth Road, Fordington, Dorchester, Dorset, 1988–9. *Proceedings of the Dorset Natural History and Archaeological Society*, 114, 19–45

Sumner, H, 1913, *The Ancient Earthworks of Cranbourne Chase*. London. Cheswick Press

Sumner, H, 1917, *The Ancient Earthworks of the New Forest*. London. Cheswick Press

Swanwick, C, (ed), 1982, *Conserving Historic Landscapes*. Castleton. Peak National Park Study Centre

Taylor, C, 1970, *Dorset*. London. Hodder and Stoughton

Taylor, C, 1974, Total archaeology. In A Rogers and T Rowley (eds) *Landscapes and Documents*. Bury St Edmunds. Standing Conference on Local History. 15–26

Thomas, J, 1993, The hermeneutics of megalithic space. In C Tilley (ed), *Interpretative Archaeology*. Oxford. Berg. 73–98

Tilley, C, 1994, *A Phenomenology of Landscape*. Oxford. Berg

Tilley, C, 1996, The power of rocks: Topography and monument construction on Bodmin Moor. *World Archaeology*, 28.2 161–176

Tuan, Y F, 1977, *Space and Place*. Minneapolis. University of Minnesota Press

Ucko, P J, Tringham, R, and Dimbleby, G W, 1972, *Man, Settlement and Urbanism*. London. Duckworth

Wainwright, G J, 1979, *Mount Pleasant, Dorset: Excavations 1970–1971* (= Reports of the Research Committee of the Society of Antiquaries of London 37). London. Society of Antiquaries

Wheatley, P, 1971, *The Pivot of the Four Quarters*. Chicago and Edinburgh. Aldine Publishing Company and Edinburgh University Press

Whittle, A, 1991, A late Neolithic complex at West Kennet, Wiltshire, England. *Antiquity*, 65, 256–62

Woodward, P, 1988, Neolithic pictures from Dorchester. *Antiquity*, 62, 266–274

Woodward, P, 1991, *The South Dorset Ridgeway: Survey and Excavations 1977–1984* (= DNHAS Monograph 8). Dorchester. Dorset Natural History and Archaeological Society

Woodward, P J, Davies, S M, and Graham, A H, 1984, Excavations on the Greyhound Yard Car Park, Dorchester, 1984. *Proceedings of the Dorset Natural History and Archaeological Society*, 106, 99–106

Woodward, P J, and Smith, R J C, 1987, Survey and excavation along the route of the Southern Dorchester Bypass, 1986–1987 – An interim note. *Proceedings of the Dorset Natural History and Archaeological Society*, 109, 79–89

7 Fish, fur and feather: Man and nature in the post-medieval landscape

Tom Williamson

Introduction

Archaeologists studying the history of the English landscape have, perhaps, paid more attention to the post-medieval period than have their colleagues working in other fields. Yet their engagement has, for the most part, been of a descriptive rather than of an explicitly theoretical character. In what follows I want to look briefly at a number of superficially unrelated changes occurring in the English landscape during the seventeenth, eighteenth and nineteenth centuries, and in so doing, show how landscape archaeology can shed light on the unwritten, and often unconscious, assumptions underlying and structuring everyday life. Specifically, I will examine how the configuration of the physical landscape can inform us about changing attitudes to nature in early modern England, and about the changing relationship between man and the natural world.

Archaeologists have sometimes posited a rather simple dichotomy between 'culture' and 'nature': a dichotomy which perhaps mirrors the recurrent disputes within the discipline itself, between social theorists and environmental archaeologists. Indeed, simple dichotomies between man and nature, between the domesticated and the natural and between farming and hunting, dominate even the most theoretically sophisticated discussions of that most important change in man/nature relations – the origins of farming. Hodder's study of the Neolithic in Europe, for example, is firmly based on a perceived dichotomy between man and nature, between *domus* and *agrios* (Hodder 1990).

Yet even a cursory examination of the historical and archaeological literature soon reveals that such simple distinctions are not universal and unchanging but, like just about everything else, are socially determined: variable from place to place and from era to era. Indeed, in many societies a neat dichotomy between hunting and domestication does not really exist. This was certainly true of England in medieval times, and throughout much of the post-medieval period, when considerable amounts of investment went in to what we might call, for want of a better term, *intermediate forms of exploitation*, that is forms of animal management which were not equivalent to the hunting of truly wild animals, nor yet to the husbandry of fully domesticated ones.

Deer, fish and pigeons

Deer farming was the most important of these strategies, and has received considerable attention from landscape archaeologists and others (Rackham 1986, 122–9; Stamper 1988; Birrell 1993). Deer parks were, in essence, specialized enclosures surrounded by a wall, fence, ditch, bank, hedge or some combination of these, intended to contain deer. The hunting and consumption of deer had been activities reserved to the élite since the earliest times, but parks were probably introduced by the Normans. Domesday Book records 35 parks, but their numbers increased inexorably in the buoyant economic conditions of the twelfth and thirteenth centuries, and by 1300 there were probably more than three thousand in England (Rackham 1986, 123). Some were attached to élite residences but the majority lay in remote locations, far from the home of the owner. Most therefore contained a 'lodge' which could provide accommodation on hunting trips, as well as serve as a base for the keeper, the official responsible for the maintenance of the park and its herds.

Parks were used for hunting but their principal function was the production of venison, the élite food *par excellence*, the food of the rich, eaten on special occasions and given as a mark of particular favour. They were, that is, specialized deer farms (Birrell 1993). But parks also fulfilled other functions. They provided grazing for pigs, cattle and horses, and produced timber and fuel, in the form of faggots from pollards and coppices (Rackham 1986, 122–9). They were, in essence, private places where the various products and facilities provided by the now dwindling 'wastes' could be shepherded, for the benefit of their élite owners: they were little slices of nature, privatized. Yet although they were in this sense 'natural' landscapes, and often developed directly from unimproved 'waste' of the manor, their principal occupants were not indigenous animals at all but the fallow deer, a European species introduced – so far as the evidence goes – around the time of the Norman Conquest.

Deer parks had a distinctive appearance which, in the more densely-settled areas of England especially, marked them out from the landscapes of more conventional agricultural production. They were largely composed of 'wood pastures', that is, areas in which animals grazed beneath closely-spaced timber trees and pollards, interspersed with open glades or *laundes* (Figure 7.1). Many also contained stands of coppiced woodland which were surrounded by banks and fences, in order to exclude the deer during the early stages of the coppice rotation (Rackham 1986, 125). Parks were expensive both to create and to maintain. In particular, the perimeter pale had to be constantly repaired, not only to keep deer in but also to keep poachers out. The latter were not necessarily the starving peasants of popular mythology. Given the peculiar status of parks as symbols of status, they were just as likely to be political rivals. Park-breaking, hunting openly in an enemy's park, was a serious affront.

In the later Middle Ages the number of parks in England declined. As the economy slumped and real wages rose in the decades following the Black Death, parks simply became too expensive for many members of the gentry. The climatic deterioration which accompanied these economic changes may also have played a part in their decline. Fallow deer, being a Mediterranean species, have little subcutaneous fat and (in terms of the English climate) an inadequate coat. The epidemics that decimated herds of cattle and flocks of sheep in the fourteenth century may well have taken their toll on deer, too. Restocking parks would have heaped an additional expense on already stretched manorial incomes (Hoppitt 1993, 132–3).

In most areas of England the number of deer parks continued to decline into the sixteenth century. But they then began to rise again. They did not, however, recover to anything approaching medieval levels and, although there were many members of the Tudor gentry who possessed a park, they were now rather more of an aristocratic privilege than had been the case in earlier centuries. More importantly, from the fifteenth century the appearance, location and significance of parks was gradually changing. No longer were they simply deer farms and hunting reserves, located in distant places. Increasingly they were being established immediately adjacent to the gentleman's residence and considered a fitting adjunct to a great house (Stamper 1988, 146–7; Woodward 1982; Prince 1967, 4–5; Thomas 1983, 202–3; Williamson 1995, 23–4). At the same time the density of trees within them was being reduced and wide areas of pasture were becoming a more prominent feature. This allowed owners and guests to enjoy extensive prospects, and thus to appreciate the full size of the park (and thus the extent of conspicuous waste involved in its creation). The wild irregularity of the park provided a pleasing contrast to the geometric order of the gardens around the house, but the principal reason for these changes was probably social. As the landed wealth of traditional feudal families was increasingly challenged by those who had made a fortune in administration, trade and the law, the possession of land, and the candid, wasteful display of that possession, became an increasingly important marker of status, and thus something to be made clearly visible at the heart of the owner's domain.

Parks provide a good example of a more general feature of 'intermediate forms of exploitation', as these developed during the late medieval and early post-medieval periods. Most involved significant investment of land or other resources, and/or the maintenance by legal sanction of a natural resource which was rare. Exploitation of the species in question was thus reserved, *de facto* or *de jure*, to the ruling élite. In turn, the structures or landscapes necessary for the maintenance of these creatures, in this case the park, themselves became, by an easy elision, signs and symbols of status, and thus something to be proudly displayed close to the home of the owner.

The maintenance of fish in purpose-built ponds was a second form of intermediate exploitation which was widespread in medieval England, and one which was again restricted to the social élite. Purpose-built fish ponds may have existed from the earliest times but, so far as the evidence goes, they gained in popularity and sophistication during the later thirteenth and fourteenth centuries, a process which culminated in the adoption of the carp (*Cyprinus carpio*) as their principal occupant; a fish which grows more rapidly, and is more hardy, than the pike and bream which had previously been the staple of the fish farmer. The carp, in an interesting parallel with deer farming, was not an indigenous species but one introduced from the Continent some time before 1400 (Currie 1991).

Fish-farming was a complex and sophisticated business, and the archaeological literature dealing with its varied remains is now fairly extensive (Aston 1988). Fish ponds come in a wide variety of forms but medieval writers made a useful distinction between the larger breeding ponds, the *vivaria* or 'great waters', which contained the principal resources of fish; and the smaller ponds, the *servatoria* or 'stews', which were used to hold the fish prior to consumption. The former were often substantial affairs, the construction of which might involve considerable feats of earth movement: most had large retaining dams and some were

Fig. 7.1. Hatfield Forest, Essex. The mixture of ancient pollards, open glades and denser stands of trees provides a good impression of the kind of wood-pasture landscape which characterised medieval deer parks.

also excavated into the natural landforms (RCHM 1982, xlvi – xlviii). They can be found in a wide variety of locations, and were often constructed within deer parks, mainly for reasons of security: manorial court rolls are full of references to illicit fishing in demesne waters. The smaller holding ponds, in contrast, were frequently found in the immediate vicinity of major ecclesiastical and lay residences, partly for reasons of security and convenience but also, perhaps, for what they proclaimed about the status of the owner. The consumption of freshwater fish, as Dyer has emphasized, was an important marker of status in medieval England (Dyer 1988).

A third form of 'intermediate exploitation' common in medieval England was the keeping of pigeons (*Columba livia*) in pigeon houses or dovecotes. *Columbaria* are frequently referred to in field names, and in medieval documents, although comparatively few medieval examples survive (Grant 1988, 186–7; Field 1993, 288). Dovecotes were a prerogative of the manorial gentry by law. 'To erect a dove house or dovecote is the right onely & badge of a lordship or signorye', as Hamon Le Strange of Hunstanton Hall in Norfolk explained in 1649 (Norfolk Record Office, Le Strange ND 22.34). The reason for this legal monopoly was simple. Pigeon flocks gorged indiscriminately on the crops growing in the surrounding fields, and thus represented a neat way of turning someone else's hard work into your own meat protein.

Like fish ponds, pigeon houses were a good source of year-round meat protein. Each pigeon produced two chicks about 8–10 times a year for around seven years. The young birds were generally culled at 4 weeks, that is, before the pin feathers had developed, and when still covered with down: the flesh was then particularly tender and juicy (Hansell 1988, 25).

Like many fish ponds, dovecotes were usually located close to the manor house. In part this was for reasons of convenience: the birds could be brought to the kitchens with relative ease. In part it was for reasons of security: raids on dovecotes were as much a feature of medieval life as was illicit fishing. In part it was because 'Dovesdunge is an excellent compost & Mucke for enriching of Grounds', as Hamon le Strange put it, and it thus made sense to position these structures close to the main garden areas. But it is also likely that dovecotes were prominently and publicly displayed because of their symbolic function. They demonstrated that the residence was a manorial hall and its owner a man of status. 'In the Middle Ages, manorial privilege was symbolized by a distinctive building which stood apart and could be seen for what it was' (Quiney 1990, 94). This symbolic role may, in part, explain the size and elaboration of the few surviving medieval examples, such as that at Leigh Court, with as many as 1,380 nesting holes, or that at Great Comberton with 1,425 (Quiney 1990, 96).

The archaeology of the rabbit

The fourth form of intermediate exploitation found in medieval England was the keeping of rabbits within warrens. Like the fallow deer, and like the carp, the rabbit (*Oryctolagus cuniculus*) was not an indigenous wild animal but a foreign immigrant, introduced, so far as the evidence goes, around the time of the Norman Conquest (Orgill 1936). The earliest archaeological evidence for its presence in this country, from the Buttermarket site at Ipswich and from Hadleigh in Essex, comes from *c*.1100 (Spencer 1956): the earliest written record is from the Scilly Isles, in 1176 (Veale 1957, 86); and probably the earliest visual representation is the carving of a dog and rabbit on a corbel of Kilpeck Church, Herefordshire, stylistically dateable to around 1160 (Rackham 1986, 47).

The rabbit was originally a semi-domesticated animal, poorly suited to our climate: various references suggest that, when transferred to a new warren, medieval rabbits would often suffer from disorientation, remaining on the surface and making no attempt to dig their own burrows. They had to be carefully nurtured and protected from predators. The earliest warrens were thus located on small islands around the coast, notably in the Scillies, on Lundy and Skokholm and in the Farne Islands (Sheial 1971, 17–18). In such locations they could also be kept away from crops as well as, more importantly, protected from poachers. But warrens were soon established in areas of coastal sand, and from the thirteenth century they were appearing inland. Some of these were extensive affairs, in marginal areas of sandy heathland, especially in the drier east of England: the East Anglian Breckland, for example, was a particularly important centre for warrening by the later fourteenth century (Bailey 1989, 131–5). More common, however, were smaller enclosures, often located close to residences, or in parks, surrounded by earthworks and fencing. These were generally referred to as *Coningers*, a term which has given rise to numerous field names, an indication of the visual impact that these features must have had in the medieval landscape. As John Field has pointed out, it was not only small fields and furlongs which were named after them, but even entire open fields; such as the *Great Felde otherwise called the Conyngrefeld* in Great Chesterton (Warwickshire), referred to in a document of 1520 (Field 1993, 73).

Gradually, the rabbit spread out from the warrens, and established independent feral colonies. As early as 1347 the lord of the manor of Petworth in Sussex, planting an orchard, purchased 2 1/2 gallons of tar for greasing the stems of the young trees 'to protect then from rabbits' (Rackham 1986, 47). Nevertheless, the animal's diffusion was slow and it was still rare in many parts of Britain as late as the eighteenth century, principally because it was so poorly adapted to local conditions. Gradual genetic mutation, together with the decline in the numbers of its principal predators, have produced the serious pest of today.

'Pillow mounds' constitute the most important archaeological monument to this widespread form of intermediate exploitation (Williamson and Loveday 1988) (Figure 7.2). These long, low, rectangular mounds, generally of equal width and height throughout, and surrounded by a shallow ditch, were first defined as a distinct class of monument by O G S Crawford in the 1920s, although they had been noted as an enigmatic feature of the landscape as early as 1877, by Canon Greenwell (Greenwell 1877, 343; Crawford 1927, 341). They have been a

Fig. 7.2. Minchinhampton, Gloucestershire. The large group of pillow mounds on Minchinhampton Common [photograph courtesy of Cambridge University Collection].

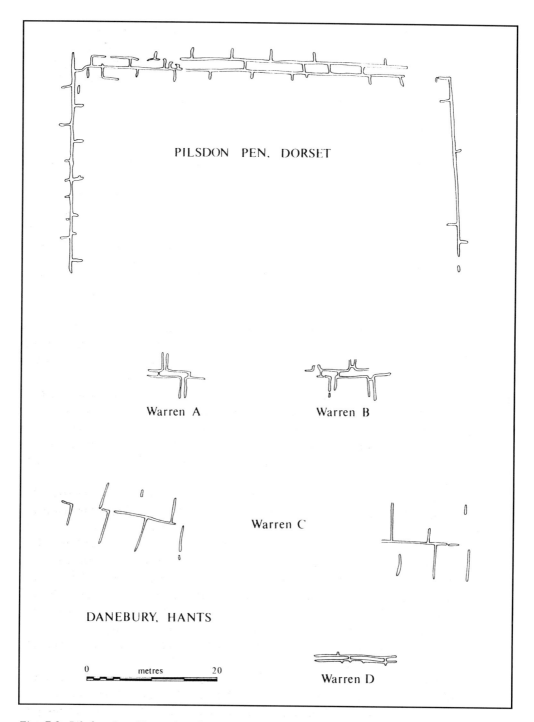

Fig. 7.3. Pilsdon Pen (Dorset) and Danebury (Hampshire). Subsoil slots, created as artificial burrows, beneath excavated pillow mounds.

source of archaeological confusion ever since, variously identified as burial mounds, prehistoric ritual features and Roman buildings (Williamson and Loveday 1988, 302–306). In part, such misidentification has resulted from the fact that early earthworks (especially hillforts) were often chosen as suitable places in which to establish warrens. But it has been compounded by the fact that – contrary to expectations – many mounds have been found on excavation to contain internal structures, principally artificial burrows. These sometimes survive in the form of slots cut into the subsoil beneath the mound – looking for all the world like beam slots or foundations trenches for a building (Gelling 1977; Cunliffe 1984, 5, 13–14) (Figure 7.3); or (in upland country) as lines of stones, which formed the capping to such slots, and which are arranged in often complex patterns beneath the mounds (RCAHM 1982, 313–45) (in addition the collapse of internal burrows sometimes leads to the appearance of slight creases or 'grooves' on the surface of the mound, a phenomenon which Crawford termed 'segmenting') (Crawford and Keiller 1928, 162). 'Pillow mound' is a modern term, coined by Crawford in the 1920s. The contemporary vernacular term for such structures, recorded in numerous documents, was some variation on 'bury', 'berrey', or 'burrow' (Williamson and Loveday 1988, 295). Pillow mounds display a bewildering degree of morphological variation, reflecting (as with fish ponds) a complex and varied form of exploitation. They come in a wide variety of sizes, can occur singly or in groups of up to eighty or more and can be linked together to make complex conjoined forms, such as crosses or squares. The fact that many were constructed in places where rabbits could happily establish themselves without their aid, in areas of very sandy soil, as for example at High Beach in Epping Forest (Warren 1926, 222), suggests that they were not intended simply to provide a suitable home for the animals in otherwise hostile environments, but also served as a method of concentrating them in easily nettable mounds. The surrounding ditches – dug down as far as the harder subsoil – prevented the creation of an extensive, rambling burrow system, and thus the proliferation of distant burrows which the warrener might not notice or net, and via which the rabbits, and perhaps the ferret, could escape unseen (Williamson and Loveday 1988, 296–300).

It is often said that pillow mounds are medieval in date, and some are. One excavated at Llanfair Clydogau (Dyfed) produced a range of radiocarbon dates centring on the fourteenth century (Austin 1988, 151). They were certainly a common feature of the landscape by the end of the sixteenth century. In 1590, in the summer assizes in Norwich, the Lord Chief Justice presided over a case concerning the title to a piece of 'bruery or heath ground' at Swainsthorpe in Norfolk. On hearing that the lords of the manor of Swainsthorpe had a warren there, he enquired whether there were 'any great and highe burrowes upon the said pece of ground such as be commonly in warrens' (Rutledge 1980). The archaeological and documentary evidence suggests, however, that the majority of surviving mounds are of seventeenth and eighteenth century date, and that some were even constructed in the nineteenth century (Williamson and Loveday 1988, 309–11; Bowen 1975, 114–7).

The warrening industry has left a number of other archaeological remains in the landscape. In the Tabular Hills of Yorkshire, on the Lincolnshire and Yorkshire Wolds and to some extent in the East Anglian Breckland, the rabbits were caught in 'types' or trapping pits, usually around 1–1.3m deep and a similar diameter across at the top. In the Tabular Hills these were lined with corbelled stone walls, and often provided with a paved floor (Harris and Spratt 1991, 185; Beastall 1978, 144). Types were placed close to a wall: a wooden tunnel, sometimes called a 'muce', ran through the wall and across the top of a pit. The pit had a tipping wooden lid which could be kept closed with wedges, allowing the rabbits to come and go freely through the wall. The types were set in enclosures c.4m to 5m square. In late summer and early autumn the rabbits were encouraged to enter the enclosure, which was filled with fodder, and during this period the trap door was kept firmly shut with a catch. In November the trap door was released, allowing as many as 400 rabbits to be caught at a time. Various other relict features sporadically survive in the landscape, most notably boundary walls, or banks of turf, like those which run for miles beneath the Forestry Commission plantations in the East Anglian Breckland, and stone-built vermin traps, a frequent feature of the Dartmoor warrens (Haynes 1970).

Rabbit warrens did not disappear at the end of the Middle Ages. Indeed, both the archaeological, and the documentary, evidence attests to the great expansion of warrens in many parts in the course of the post-medieval period, and especially from the mid seventeenth century. They were a particular feature of chalk Wolds and Downland areas, but they were also important in many forests, and in some upland regions. On Dartmoor, for example, large-scale warrenning seems to have developed in the second half of the seventeenth century, while on the Tabular Hills in Yorkshire the years around 1700 saw a major expansion of what had formerly been a small-scale industry (Harris and Spratt 1991, 198–9).

'Intermediate exploitation' in the post-medieval period

Rabbit warrens were not the only form of intermediate exploitation which remained important, or even increased in importance, in the early modern period. We often think of parks, ponds and dovecotes as essentially *medieval* phenomena, but in fact they continued to flourish during the post-medieval centuries, and especially in the decades after 1660. One important aspect of this was the increase in the number of deer parks following the Restoration (Williamson 1995, 24, 46–7). In many parts of the country, especially the Midlands and south east, the century after 1660 saw, perhaps, twice as many new creations as had taken place over the previous hundred years. In Thirsk's words, 'the gentry seem to have lost much of their interest in deer parks and deer keeping in the course of the late sixteenth and early seventeenth centuries. Their enthusiasm revived after 1660' (1985a, 367).

The keeping of pigeons likewise 'aroused fresh interest after 1660' (Thirsk 1985b, 575–6): the majority of surviving dovecotes seem to have been erected between c.1660 and c.1750 (Barley 1985, 647; Whitworth 1993). And fish ponds were enthusiastically maintained, and were a subject of élite discourse, into the eighteenth century (Thirsk 1985b, 576). No less a figure than Roger North, the noted mathematician and architect, published a treatise on the subject in 1713 (North 1713). A series of legislative acts was passed in the later seventeenth century protecting these traditional forms of exploitation from poaching and vandalism. That of 1670 protected deer parks, rabbit warrens and fish ponds from all poachers with guns, snares and nets.

Moreover, these traditional forms of exploitation were joined in the Restoration period by new ones, the most significant of which was the duck decoy (Payne Galwey 1886; Wentworth Day 1954, 115–7). Decoys consisted of a number of curving 'pipes' – tapering channels covered by netting and supported on a framework of hoops – leading off from an area of open water. These were typically about a hundred metres long, and twenty metres wide at the mouth. Each pipe terminated in a long bow-net which could be detached from the rest of the apparatus. Along one or both sides of the pipe a number of screens, usually made of reeds, were arranged *en echelon*: behind these the decoy man could conceal himself. Wildfowl were usually lured in to the pipe by using a combination of tame decoy ducks and a specially trained dog called a 'piper'. The former were trained to enter the pipe when commanded to do so by a low whistle from the decoyman. The dog would, at the same time, run around the screens, jumping over lower boards or 'dog jumps' placed between them. For reasons which have never been fully explained, the wild-fowl which had gathered near the mouth of the pipe were attracted towards what must, to them, have looked like an appearing and disappearing dog. This, plus the example set by the tame decoy ducks, induced them to swim up the pipe. As soon as they had entered, the decoyman – who had up to this time remained well hidden – revealed himself. By waving his arms or a handkerchief the birds were scared into flight down the tapering pipe, and into the bow-net, which could then be disconnected from the rest of the structure and the birds despatched (Patterson 1909, 11–8).

In one sense decoys are rather different from the various kinds of semi-domestication which we have been discussing so far. They were more akin to true hunting, for the wildfowl were not confined by physical barriers within a defined area, nor regularly supplied with food, as was the case – to varying extents – with deer, pigeons, carp and rabbits. But in another sense they are part of the same general phenomenon, in that they involved considerable investment in plant and equipment, and major alterations to the landscape. Decoys are sometimes said to have been introduced from Holland after the Glorious Revolution of 1688. In fact, some had been established before the Civil War. Sir William Wodehouse had, as early as 1620, a 'device for catching DUCKS, known by the foreign name of a koye' at Waxham in Norfolk (Payne Galwey 1886, 2). Those at Acle and Hemsby in the same county were probably established at about the same time (Baker 1985, 1), while that at Purdis Farm in Suffolk was in existence by 1646, when it was referred to in a lease (East Suffolk Record Office HA 93/3/48). Flixton Decoy in the same county was in full operation by 1652, when it was carefully drawn on an estate map (East Suffolk Record Office 295) (Figure 7.4). Nevertheless, while some were established before the Restoration around the coastal marshes of Norfolk and Suffolk, their numbers seem to have increased here after 1660, and at the same time they spread into the adjacent counties of Cambridgeshire, Essex and Lincolnshire. By 1724, travelling through north western Cambridgeshire, Daniel Defoe was able to describe how:

> In these fens are abundance of those admirable pieces of art called duckoys; that is to say, places so adapted for the harbour and shelter of wild-fowl, and then furnished with a breed of those they call decoy-ducks ... (Defoe 1724, 101)

Decoys always remained a speciality of East Anglia and the adjacent areas, but they were sporadically constructed elsewhere (Thirsk 1985b, 576). There were a number in Somerset, on Sedgemoor and beside the Severn (as at Berkley); a handful in Yorkshire and Cheshire, and even in Dorset, like the famous example at Abbotsbury. As with post-medieval rabbit warrens, decoys were operated on a variety of scales. Some were relatively small affairs, which simply supplied the domestic requirements of their gentlemen owners. Others were, or became, large-scale ventures, leased out to commercial operators. Defoe, describing the Fenland decoys in 1707, remarked how:

> It is incredible what quantities of wild-fowl of all sorts, duck, mallard, teal, widgeon &c. they take in those duckoys every week, during the season. It may indeed be guessed at a little by this, that there is a duckoy not far from Ely, from which they assured me at St Ives (a town on the Ouse, where the fowl they took was always brought to be sent to London) that they generally sent up three thousand couple a week. (Defoe 1724, 101)

Such a quantity was, according to Defoe, said to have been worth £500 a year in rent. To some extent differences in the scale and nature of these enterprises is reflected in morphological variation. While some decoys had only two or three pipes, others had as many as twenty. Some decoys were arranged around a purpose-built area of water, others – and especially the earlier ones – made use of natural lakes and meres.

Decoys have not left such clear traces in the modern landscape as rabbit warrens. Once abandoned, the pipes – and often the open water of the pond itself – rapidly became colonized with vegetation: first by reeds, subsequently by alder carr. However, the decoy generally lives on in the names it has given to neighbouring features in the countryside: names such as Decoy Farm, Decoy Plantation, Decoy Wood, Decoy Carr or Decoy Covert. Field names, too, sometimes preserve their memory: examples include Coy Ducks in Brindley, Cheshire, Decoy Meadow in Mouldsworth in the same county and Decoy Field, in Tolleshunt D'Arcy and in Wormingford (both in Essex) (Field 1993, 77). Their prominence in contemporary mental geography is indicated by the fact that eighteenth-century small-scale county maps, such as those produced for Suffolk by Emmanuel Bowen in 1764, show decoys with as much prominence as they show deer parks, churches or country towns.

The archaeological and documentary evidence thus suggests that the period from the mid seventeenth to the mid eighteenth century represented, in many ways, the heyday of these various forms of 'intermediate exploitation'. It was certainly a period in which they were developed with renewed enthusiasm by rural landowners. This is an intriguing phenomenon, and one which demands some explanation. In part, as Joan Thirsk has argued, it was probably due to economic factors (Thirsk 1985a, 366–8; 1985b, 575–7). Population growth slackened after 1650, and remained sluggish until the 1750s; agricultural prices, especially those for cereals, consequently remained relatively low. In such a climate landowners were keen to invest in new activities: investment in warrens, decoys or whatever represented, in other words, a form of agricultural diversification. Yet it is also possible to argue that there were important *social* reasons for the resurgence of interest in these various forms of intermediate exploitation. During the Civil War and Interregnum they had come under sustained attack, in part for what they symbolized – established rank and privilege. Thus a group of Parliamentary

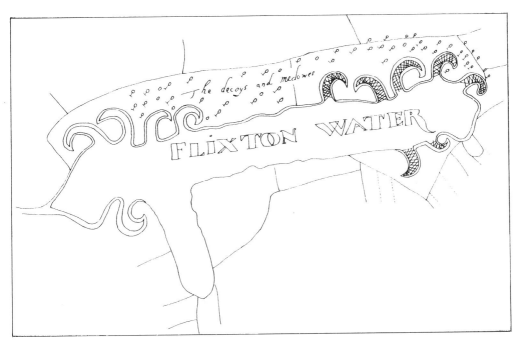

Fig. 7.4. The duck decoy at Flixton, Suffolk, as shown on an estate map of 1652; one of the earliest known representations of a decoy.

soldiers, stationed at Leamington, did considerable damage to Baron Trevor's dovecote. When their commanding officer remonstrated with them they replied that:

> Pigeons were fowls of the air given to the sons of men, and all men had a common right
> in them that could get them, and they were as much theirs as the barons, and therefore
> they would kill them ... and not part from their right: upon which the captain said he was
> so convinced by their arguments he could not answer them, and so came away, letting
> them do as they would... (Thomas 1983, 49)

In the 1640s Parliament debated the abolition of the manorial monopoly on the keeping of pigeons; one commentator argued that it would be a:

> Blemish of government that the enferiour sort of people should assume that power and
> libertye wch in reason and policye of state ought to belonge to great estates and persons
> of qualitye and commision. (Norfolk Record Office Le Strange ND 22.34).

Deer parks in particular were both a target for generalized vandalism on the part of army radicals, and of more systematic asset-stripping on the part of the revolutionary government, as deer were sold and timber was felled on the property of sequestered royalists. Hardly surprising, then, that in the period of stability following this phase of mid-century social upheaval all these traditional, quintessential symbols of gentry status enjoyed renewed

Fig. 7.5. Averham Park, Nottinghamshire, c. 1730. The house, built within an existing deer park as a second home by Lord Lexington c. 1725, overlooks the family seat at nearby Kelham. Note the open fields ploughed in ridges in the foreground, and preserved as ridge and furrow under the parkland grass.

popularity; nor that they were, perhaps more than ever before, closely associated with the residential complex and – in many cases – embellished accordingly.

Thus after 1660 the deer park's function as the prestigious setting for a country house was triumphant. Only very rarely were they now created or maintained at any distance from a major residence. When they were, the lodge itself tended to mutate into a private retreat, a secondary residence, as at Averham in Nottinghamshire (Figure 7.5). Here in the 1720s Lord Lexington erected a particularly elaborate lodge within the park which served as a kind of second home, overlooking the main family residence at nearby Kelham (Barley 1985, 617). The ease and effectiveness with which a park could be created was now a vital factor in deciding where a gentleman might build a new house. Thus in 1670 John Evelyn described how he helped choose the site for a friend's new house at Burrough Green in Cambridgeshire, and they selected 'a spot, on a rising ground, & adorn'd with venerable woods, a dry and sweete prospect East and West, and fit for a Parke' (De Beer 1955a, 553).

What was true of the park was also true of the other structures and facilities associated with 'intermediate exploitation'. Dovecotes not only continued to be erected in large numbers in the late seventeenth and early eighteenth centuries. They were also prominently positioned, as in earlier centuries, often forming part of the ornamental gardens; and they were increasingly elaborate structures, their fine architectural detailing demonstrating their more than utilitarian nature (Hansell 1988). Fishponds, too, were objects of beauty as much as production. As Roger North made clear, they should be located close to the house:

Whereby you may with little Trouble, and at any Time, take out all or any Fish they contain: therefore it is good to place them in some inclos'd Ground near the chief Mansion House. Some Recess in a Garden is very proper, because the Fish are fenc'd from Robbers, and your Journey to them is Short and easy, and your Eye will be often upon them, which will conduce to their being well kept... (North 1713, 21)

But in addition, as North emphasized, in such a position they contributed to the beauty of the house's setting, and would be 'an Ornament to the Walks'. Indeed, as Chris Currie has emphasized, most of the ornamental basins and canals which were such a feature of late seventeenth- and early eighteenth-century gardens also served as fish stews (Curie 1990). Significantly, North stressed the recreational side of fish keeping:

There is Advantage enough in the Mastery of Fish, from the Diversion, not to speak of the Employment that it brings to a family. Young People love Angling extremely: then there is a Boat, which gives Pleasure enough in Summer, frequent fishing with Nets, the very making of Nets, seeing the Waters, much Discussion of them, and the Fish, especially upon your great Sweeps, and the strange Surprises that will happen in Numbers and Bigness, with many other incident entertainments, are the Result of Waters, and direct the Minds of a numerous Family to terminate in something not inconvenient, and it may divert them from worse. (North 1713, 72–3)

This passage clearly expresses the complex mixture of status display, recreation, utilitarian production and aesthetics associated with fish ponds in this period. Sometimes the larger ponds, the 'great waters' which were located at a distance from the principal residence, became a focus for a detached garden area. Somerleyton Hall in Suffolk was equipped with very elaborate gardens by 1652, when they are depicted on an estate map and described in a written survey. But there was also a separate, isolated area of pleasure grounds which lay some 1.25 kilometres to the south of the hall, outside the park altogether, and separated from it by an area of arable fields. These gardens were arranged around two large fish ponds, probably in origin 'broads', that is, lakes created by the flooding of medieval turbaries. The survey describes how:

The Lady Wentworth hath...divers fish ponds gardens and walks with a house in farm ... the waters called the Island Pond and the Wall Pond they are outward lying being part in Somerleyton part in Blundeston. There is likewise one other great area of water that is also a private water of the said Lady Wentworth called Dole Fenn with walks and mounts dividing lying part in Somerleyton and part in Blundeston. (East Suffolk Record Office 942.64 Som)

Other forms of intermediate exploitation also took their place close to the residences of the gentry. Even rabbit warrens might sometimes be so located: Stephen Switzer advocated the establishment of fenced warrens as a feature of gardens in his *Ichnographica Rustica* of 1718 (Switzer 1718, 98). More usually, however, they were placed a little distance away in the adjacent parkland, presumably to avoid damage to garden crops. In a similar way, decoys were seldom located close to residences, in this case because the birds were easily scared away by noise and activity. But they, too, were often placed in parks, or otherwise within easy reach of the gentleman's house. In 1681 John Evelyn visited Mr Denzil Onslow of Pyrford in Surrey and described

> Such an extraordinary feast ... there was not any thing, save what his estate about it did afford; as Venison, Rabbts, hairs, Pheasants, Partridges, Pigeons, Quale, Poultrie, all sorts of fowle in season (from his own decoy nere his house) ... all sorts of fresh fish. After dinner we went to see sport at the decoy. (De Beer 1955, 255)

This quotation says it all. Productive facilities like fish ponds and dovecotes, along with enclosed gardens and orchards loaded with fruit, had an aesthetic appeal because they proclaimed, in a world dogged by dearth, the fact that the owner ate varied and exotic food in abundance, and was fully involved in the productive administration of his estate (Williamson 1985, 31–5). Indeed, the gentry's involvement in such pursuits – on a recreational or a commercial basis – was part and parcel of a more general phenomenon of the Restoration period. Poets and essayists continually emphasized the virtues of a life devoted to estate administration and farming, to useful production. Moreover, the produce of deer parks, fish ponds, warrens, decoys and pigeon houses – like the exotic fruit from the garden – was frequently given as gifts to neighbours: they formed part of the complex web of reciprocal obligations which helped bind rural society together. 'You may oblige your Friends and neighbours', wrote North, 'by making Presents of your fish, which, from the Countryman to the King, is well taken' (North 1713, 56). Indeed, many country house archives from this period contain books listing the presents made to, and received by, landowners. Deer remained the élite gift *par excellence*, however: Robert Walpole kept a 'deer book' in which he listed the various gifts of venison from the park at Houghton in Norfolk which he doled out to political allies, and what was received, in terms of votes in the House, or political support in elections, in return.

The archaeological and documentary evidence thus attest the continuing importance of the various intermediate forms of exploitation well into the post-medieval period, and suggest that there was renewed interest in them, on the part of English landowners, in the period after the Civil War. Indeed, in many ways the period *c.*1660–1750 represented the heyday of warrens, decoys, dovecotes and fishponds. In part, as Joan Thirsk has suggested, this enthusiasm was the consequence of straightforward economic considerations – the stagnation of the conventional agrarian economy consequent on slow or negative demographic growth. But it was also, as I have argued, the result of important social forces, and represented the assertion of traditional symbols of privilege after a period of revolutionary upheaval.

The decline of intermediate exploitation 1750–1850

But all this was to change in the century after 1750. Gradually, inexorably, the various forms of intermediate exploitation declined in both social and in economic importance. Rabbit warrens, in particular, came under attack. Castigated as wasteful and archaic by agricultural improvers, their numbers dwindled noticeably in areas of light chalk wolds and downland, especially in the decades either side of 1800. By the end of the nineteenth century commercial warrens were largely restricted to areas where the soils were particularly marginal for agriculture, such as the upland moors of south Wales, or Dartmoor. Thus in Yorkshire, on the poor soils of the Tabular Hills, some warrens continued to operate throughout the nineteenth and even into the twentieth century; but their numbers dwindled on the more fertile Wolds (as they did in neighbouring Lincolnshire) from the end of the eighteenth century, due to agricultural improvements and the progressive conversion of grassland to arable (Harris and Spratt 1991, 201; Beastall 1978, 145). At the same time, small-scale domestic warrens were going out of fashion. Dovecotes went the same way: the gentry began to lose interest in the 1760s and 70s. Comparatively few new examples were erected in the second half of the eighteenth century, and while some existing structures were maintained, many were demolished: they were of little real importance by the middle years of the nineteenth century. The decline of duck decoys came slightly later, but was noticeable by the 1830s. By the end of the century only two decoys on the Norfolk Broads were still in operation (at Fritton and Barnaby) and decoying had effectively come to an end in the Fenlands (Dutt 1903, 115–18).

Declining interest in these traditional forms of animal exploitation is nowhere more evident than in the changing setting of the country house. For garden historians, the second half of the eighteenth century is, above all, the age of 'Capability' Brown, in which walled gardens and enclosures were stripped away from the house so that it could stand within open parkland, the turf appearing to flow right up to its walls (Stroud 1965; Turner 1985; Taigel and Williamson 1993, 65–81). What is not always sufficiently emphasized is that when the walled formal gardens were swept away, so too were barns, farmyards and other productive facilities, including, of course, such things as fish ponds and dovecotes. Moreover, the parkland itself was undergoing a further transition in appearance and function. The number of parks increased rapidly to the extent that by 1800 virtually all landowners of any consequence had their homes set within one. But aesthetics now completely dominated their design. While these *landscape parks* derived many of their basic features from the 'traditional' deer park – turf, scattered trees – they were tidied up, manicured. Most significantly of all, only a small proportion had deer kept within them. In part, this was because of the expense involved in feeding the deer over the winter, and in repairing the pale, for the majority of landscape parks newly created in this period belonged to the local gentry, rather than to the greatest landowners. In part, it was because deer damaged young planting, and thus as the *aesthetic* role of the park increased, the importance of deer within them declined. But it also indicates a marked reduction in the importance of deer as symbols of status. Indeed, even some long-established deer parks, owned by great landed families, lost their deer in this period, to be replaced by 'improved' breeds of sheep or cattle.

Of course, we should not exaggerate the speed with which the gentry marginalized the older forms of exploitation from their aesthetic landscapes. Most of the serpentine lakes in landscape parks, for example, were stocked with fish. Well into the nineteenth century new decoys were occasionally constructed, like that at Titchmarsh in Northamptonshire, built in 1885 (RCHM 1975); like dovecotes – which also experienced a minor revival in mid-century – these were often the creation of 'new men' who had made their money in trade and industry. As such they were badges of antiquarian status, somewhat self-consciously adopted. By this time there was no serious interest in warrens or decoys, fish ponds or rabbit warrens. They were a marginalized aspect of the economy, and had ceased to be an essential feature of the landscape of gentility.

The reasons for the slow decline in the intermediate forms of exploitation are complex, but appear to have been inextricably linked to three inter-related developments which continued through the later eighteenth and early nineteenth centuries; demographic expansion, the development of a more complex and commercial society, and improvements in agriculture. Demographic growth resumed in the middle decades of the eighteenth century, agricultural prices rose and with them farm rents and the incomes of landowners (hence, of course, the proliferation of parks and their rapid diffusion down the social scale to the level of the parish gentry). The second half of the eighteenth century consequently saw increased levels of investment in agriculture, large-scale schemes of enclosure and reclamation, and a wave of agricultural innovation. All this had a number of effects.

Firstly, with the increased use of artificial grasses (clover, nonsuch) and turnips as fodder, larger numbers of domestic stock could be kept through the winter, and this reduced the attraction of carp, pigeons and the rest as a source of seasonal fresh meat. Secondly, and more significantly, many of these forms of intermediate exploitation had represented ways of using land which, in the economic and technological conditions prevailing before the mid eighteenth century, had been highly marginal for more conventional forms of agrarian production. This was particularly true of rabbit warrens, which were often located in areas of acid heathland. Warrens also had the additional advantage that they could be established by manorial lords in areas of unenclosed common land, the dominant form of land use in such terrain. In the new age of agricultural improvement, however, these areas could often be reclaimed through enclosure and intensive marling; the heaths were ploughed and the rabbits destroyed. In a similar way, improved drainage of wetlands and marshes, associated with the adoption of more sophisticated forms of drainage windmill and, in the nineteenth century, steam pumps, reduced the numbers of wildfowl in the environment and thus the quantities which could be caught in decoys, making them a less viable proposition.

Indeed, what distinguished this phase of 'Agricultural Revolution' from earlier periods of agrarian innovation, in the sixteenth and seventeenth centuries, was the extent of the inroads being made into the remaining wild areas of England; environments which, as *we* now know but contemporaries generally did not, were semi-natural, largely anthropogenic in origin. Upland moors, lowland heaths and commons all came under assault, with vast tracts being enclosed by Parliamentary Acts, especially in the period of the Napoleonic Wars (Turner 1980). In more subtle ways, too, nature was being tamed. In the long-enclosed areas, in the old wood-pasture farming regions, field boundaries were being removed or realigned, and thousands of timber trees and pollards felled. Moreover, through under-draining – widespread over much of lowland England by the 1770s – and by the intensive marling of acid land, the very soil chemistry of England was being transformed, on an unprecedented scale. This was, indeed, an age of Agricultural Revolution.

It is thus tempting to argue that the old forms of 'intermediate exploitation' were simply victims of circumstances, archaic practices rendered redundant by agricultural innovation and environmental change, casualties of the modern economic world. Yet this is too simple. To begin with, changing patterns of land use can hardly explain the gentry's growing disenchantment with fish ponds and dovecotes. We should note that such activities were not only marginalized in commercial terms, but also in aesthetic and recreational terms. Regency gentlemen would not normally adjourn after supper to observe the working of a decoy, or to stroll around the estate fish ponds. More importantly, we should not assume that the improving zeal of landowners was simply based on hard-nosed economic considerations, or was even economically rational. Indeed, many attempts at land reclamation were wildly optimistic ventures which had little real chance of financial success. Thus, for example, on the East Anglian Breckland the late eighteenth century saw large-scale attempts at enclosure and improvement, but the heaths were ploughed and the warrens were destroyed to no avail. Much of the new arable land here had tumbled back down to grass even before the end of the Napoleonic Wars. 'Improvement' in such environments was often seen as an end in itself, a duty, a mission. When in 1774 Thomas de Grey bemoaned the costs of enclosing the heaths at Tottington in Breckland, he observed candidly that the 'great expense ... would but ill answer, unless there was a real satisfaction in employing the labourers and bringing forth a ragged dirty parish to a neatness of cultivation' (Norfolk Record Office, Walsingham WLS XXLVII/19 415 X 5).

Landowners were thus deeply involved in the 'improvement' of their estates. But such activities expressed a subtly different set of values than those implicit in the lifestyle of an earlier generation. In the seventeenth and early eighteenth centuries gentlemen had taken some pride in the closeness of their involvement in the affairs of estate management and husbandry; their diaries and memoranda books record their brewing activities, the fruit in their gardens, the size of their sows' litters. By the end of the century their involvement was more managerial, more *distanced*. Their estate landscapes reflected this. The productive clutter of gardens, yards, orchards and fishponds which had formerly swarmed around country houses was replaced by the sweeping, elegant simplicity of the landscape park. In this affluent, leisured age, gentlemen took more interest in shopping and assemblies than they did in horticulture and fish keeping. In a society characterized by rampant consumerism, superior resources of *production* were no longer a sign of distinction. Of course, as I have argued elsewhere, parks had another, more profound social significance (Williamson 1995, 100–140). The movement of settlements and the diversion of roads, the planting of dense perimeter belts, also reflected the increased social polarization in the eighteenth-century countryside, the withdrawal of landowners from the local community. They were private places for the entertainment of the 'polite', and as such, as Robert Williams has emphasized, they continued to operate as a 'private larder ... a sylvan arena for blood sports' (Williams 1987, 81) (Figures 7.6 and 7.7).

Indeed, it is a striking paradox that, at precisely the same time as they were throwing more and more of their energies into land improvement schemes, reclaiming wildernesses and changing nature, landowners were also increasingly interested in, indeed, obsessed by, the most natural form of food procurement – hunting. This we may define, in an eighteenth-century context, as the taking of animals and birds which, while they might be encouraged in the environment, were not constrained within enclosures or permanently housed. They were pursued more for recreation than as a source of food. Significantly, the quarry could not always be eaten: it was in the period after 1750 that fox-hunting became a particularly

Fig. 7.6. The Duke of Newcastle Returning from Shooting, by Francis Wheatley 1788. The painting is set – appropriately enough – in the park at Clumber, and the ornamental parkland bridge can be seen in the background.

serious matter of polite recreation, rather than of parochial pest-control (Carr 1976).

The hunting of game birds, hares and rabbits had been a feature of upper-class life since medieval times. But in the course of the post-medieval period, and particularly in the wake of the Restoration, it was an activity increasingly reserved to the landed rich. By the terms of the Game Act of 1671, hares, rabbits and game birds could only be taken by people possessing freehold property worth at least £100 per year, holding leaseholds of 99 years or longer or copyholds worth at least £150 a year. The right to hunt, even on a person's own land, was thus restricted to less than 1 per cent of the population. Increasing interest in maintaining game is attested by subsequent acts, in 1707 and – in particular – in 1723. The notorious Black Act of this date, 'for the more effectual punishment of wicked and evil-disposed persons going armed, in disguise', laid down that merely appearing in the vicinity of a game reserve, armed and with face blackened, was a hanging offence (Munsche 1981, 8–27).

Yet while the gentry's interest in hunting and game-preservation was already strong in

Fig. 7.7. 18th century game card from Blenheim. Such cards, which accompanied gifts of game, often indicate the importance of the park as the main game preserve on a great estate. Dead pheasants, woodcocks and hare in the foreground; the park and the Column of Victory in the distance [by kind permission of His Grace the Duke of Marlborough].

the first half of the century, it increased steadily after *c*.1750, with considerable effects upon the landscape. As the English countryside became more enclosed, and as landed estates became increasingly consolidated, more strenuous attempts could be made to preserve game, safe in the knowledge that the birds would not simply wander off onto a neighbour's land. Game books show that the average size of the estate 'bag' steadily rose throughout the second half of the eighteenth century, especially on the larger estates, despite the repeated claims of contemporaries that game was becoming scarcer. An increase in the opportunities for game preservation was accompanied by improvements in firearm technology which ensured that ever larger numbers could be shot. Through the 1750s, 60s and 70s guns became lighter and shorter, and in 1782 William Watts, a Bristol plumber, discovered how to make 'drop shot', by pouring molten lead in a coarse spray from the top of a tower: this solidified into fairly accurate spheres as it descended, creating shot which penetrated further into the body of the prey. In 1787, the London gun maker Henry Nock invented the 'patent breech', which had a hole running right through the stock to the middle of the charge, rather than along its edge (Hastings 1969). Because it thus ignited the charge from the middle outwards, the explosion was much faster and considerably more powerful. These changes ensured further reductions in the length of gun barrels, dropping from an average of 3′6″ in 1760 to 2′6″ in 1790. Guns could be lighter, more manoeuvrable and thus better suited to aerial slaughter.

As the availability of game and the accuracy of guns increased, the ability of sportsmen increasingly came to be judged by their marksmanship, most conveniently measured by the number of birds that they could bring down. This in turn gave further encouragement to the idea that shooting flying birds, which involved greater personal skill, was of prime importance. In 1770 the idea that 'gentlemen shoot flying' was strongly propagated in the book *The Art of Shooting-Flying*; by 1801 the author of the standard text on field sports noted that it was 'not exactly at present the custom for Gentlemen to shoot on the ground' (Page 1784). By this time, the increasingly competitive nature of the sport meant that large numbers of players were often now involved, frequently groups of guests invited to come specifically to enjoy the pleasures of the shoot. Further improvements in firearms technology, and in particular the invention of the detonator in 1807, allowed further refinements: the development of true 'battue' shooting in which beaters would drive the birds out of the covert, and into sight of the waiting line of sportsmen.

The second half of the eighteenth century thus saw fundamental changes in the practice of game shooting. In 1750 it had been a casual, rather leisurely pastime involving two or three friends, accompanied by dogs, taking pot-shots at birds on the ground or near to it. By 1800 it was a far more organized activity, involving much larger numbers of people shooting large numbers of birds in full flight. The native partridge, which had been the principal quarry on most estates in the first half of the eighteenth century, was not well suited to this new form of shooting: it spent much of its time on the ground and, when scared into flight, flew low across the fields. Nor was it well suited to being raised in large numbers, for it had (and has) large territories, as much as ten acres to a pair of birds in the winter. Far better suited to the new demands was the pheasant. Not only did this occupy much smaller territories. It also flew high:

> *Phasianus colchinus* shot up over the tree-tops like a rocket, its long tail flaunting, its cocketting cry an incitement to the sportsman below. (Hopkins 1985, 68)

Systematic attempts at rearing pheasants for shooting began in the early eighteenth century but only really took off after 1750. 'Pheasantries' began to be constructed in which eggs found on the estate were hatched under domestic hens, and the young chicks then suitably pampered, fed on chopped boiled eggs, ants eggs, and even toast soaked in urine. The brood was treated like this until ready to be set out in the woods.

At the same time greater and greater efforts were made to curb the bird's natural predators, hawks, owls, weasels, crows, stoats, magpies, polecats and foxes, and to control a massive increase in the incidence of poaching, a development directly related to the increase in the scale of the temptation now offered to the poor, the hungry or the criminal by the gentry's well-stocked coverts. A series of Acts, prescribing increasingly severe penalties, culminated in the Night Poaching Act of 1817, which prescribed seven years transportation to any person caught, suitably equipped for poaching, in 'any forest, chase, park, wood, plantation, close or other open or enclosed ground' (Munsche 1981, 76–105).

All this legislative activity was to little avail, however. When in 1831 the archaic property qualifications for hunting were finally abolished (and the sale of game again legalized) around a sixth of all convictions in England were for game law offences. Most estates were in a state of permanent siege against poachers, and took their own, vicious, measures to protect game, in particular by placing man-traps in the plantations, and mounting patrols by groups of keepers at night.

The gentry's obsession with the pheasant had profound effects on the landscape. The pheasant, unlike the partridge, was only really at home in woodland, and where this did not exist it had to be planted. Indeed, the need for pheasant cover was a major, if not *the* major, motivation behind the extensive schemes of afforestation carried out by landed estates in the second half of the eighteenth century. But the particular habits and proclivities of the pheasant also helped determine the configuration and layout of plantations. Pheasants need woods but they do not live in their depths. As Blaine put it in 1858, pheasants 'are generally found in woody places, on the borders of plains where they delight to sport' (Blaine 1858, 808): in other words they are essentially a creature of the woodland edge. Indeed, a modern study of radio-tagged birds revealed that they spend almost all their time within 20 metres of the boundary between woodland and open ground (Hill and Robertson 1988, 43). As the same study noted, this preference has an important effect on the holding capacity of woods of different size or shape. Small woods, by their very nature, have a higher edge to area ratio, and the optimum size for a covert would be less than a hectare. The ratio could be further improved, for obvious reasons, by ensuring that the woods were ovoid or circular in shape. A large number of small woods would also allow the maximum number of pheasants to gain territories at breeding time. Large, continuous blocks of woodland, in contrast, often contain areas which are far from any woodland edge and thus of little use to pheasants (Hill and Robertson 1988, 43). The only big woods suitable for intensive pheasant rearing are, therefore, ones planted in the form of a long thin strip, especially if provided with sinuous or scalloped edges. Such considerations not only helped determine the layout of much of the estate woodland established in this period. They also helped structure the basic planting within the landscape park, the principal game reserve on most estates: the small clumps and thin perimeter belts which were the hallmark of the Brownian style made ideal cover (Figure 7.8).

The gentry, then, were obsessed with pheasant; with shooting it in ever-larger numbers, with preventing any one else from doing so. And they also continued, of course, to shoot partridges, hares, rabbits and a host of wildfowl on an ever-increasing scale, and to ride in pursuit of the fox. Sport had always been important: but now it became central to country life. This increasing importance of hunting and shooting, and the decline of various forms of 'intermediate exploitation', were intimately connected. In part this connection was a direct one; the needs of hunting in some cases conflicted directly with their operation. Decoys, for example, needed peace and quiet to work effectively. The increased popularity of wildfowl shooting in wetland areas from the late eighteenth century brought recurrent complaints that decoys were suffering. Similarly, in many areas of light acid soils the maintenance of rabbit warrens came into conflict with the needs of pheasant-shooting, because rabbits systematically destroyed the plantations necessary to establish viable populations of the birds. Of more importance, however, were the *indirect* effects which the enthusiasm for hunting and shooting brought about; especially when combined with the

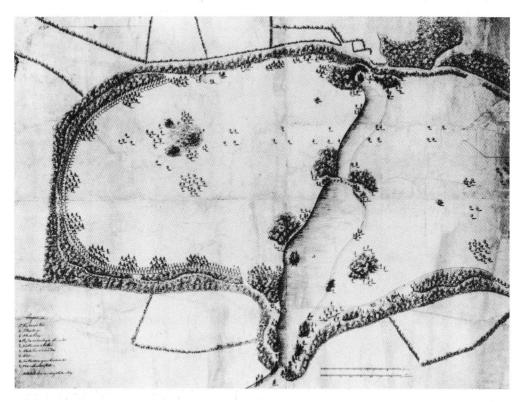

Fig. 7.8. Typical parkland planting: Capability Brown's design for the North Park, Wimpole, 1767. Thin belts and small clumps made ideal pheasant cover.

landowners' equally obsessive interest in agricultural innovation and land improvement. As I have already intimated, there was a paradox and an implicit conflict here: on the one hand nature was to be controlled and improved, wild places to be tamed and the wilderness eradicated. On the other hand, the hunting of wild animals, and their careful, ruthless preservation so that they could be hunted, became *the* central concern of rural life. In the face of these contrary pressures, it is not surprising that gentlemen began to lose interest in 'intermediate forms of exploitation'. They felt uneasy with them, for they could no longer be fitted easily into the conceptual categories which dominated their lives and their discourse. Nature and culture were becoming increasingly polarized, at least in the minds of the wealthy. Hunting was one thing, an agreeable recreational activity with important social functions, binding together the upper strata of society. Farming and estate improvement were another: profitable activities, socially responsible, and respectable enough, at least if undertaken at arms' length. But the two could no longer be combined as a single activity by the 'polite'. It was this profound shift, combined with the more straightforward environmental and economic changes already outlined, which led to the demise of intermediate forms of exploitation in the century after 1750.

This is, of course, only one of many threads running through the history of the post-medieval rural landscape. But there is an important story to tell here, about subtle changes in human attitudes to nature, and about the ordering and definition of human experience. And like many such stories, it is, perhaps, more clearly inscribed in the archaeology of the landscape than it is in written texts. Landscape archaeology has as much to tell us, I would argue, about the development of society in the seventeenth, eighteenth, or nineteenth centuries, as it has about those more remote periods of time which are the concern of other contributors to this volume.

Bibliography

Aston, M, (ed), 1988, *Medieval Fish, Fisheries and Fish Ponds in England* (= BAR British Series 182). Oxford. British Archaeological Reports. (2 vols.)

Austin, D, 1988, Excavation and survey at Bryn Cysegrfan, Llanfair Clydogau, Dyfed 1979. *Medieval Archaeology*, 12, 130 – 165

Bailey, M, 1989, *A Marginal Economy? East Anglian Breckland in the Later Middle Ages*. Cambridge. Cambridge University Press

Baker, R E, 1985, Norfolk duck decoys. *Transactions of the Norfolk and Norwich Naturalists Society*, 27.1, 1–8

Barley, M, 1985, Rural Buildings in England. In J Thirsk (ed), *The Agrarian History of England and Wales. Volume 2.1: 1640–1750*. Cambridge. Cambridge University Press. 590–685

Beastall, T W, 1978, *The Agricultural Revolution in Lincolnshire*. Lincoln. Society for Lincolnshire History and Archaeology

Beer, E S De, (ed), 1955a, *The Diary of John Evelyn. Volume 3*. Oxford. Oxford University Press

Beer, E S De, (ed), 1955b, *The Diary of John Evelyn. Volume 4*. Oxford. Oxford University Press

Birrell, J, 1993, Deer and deer farming in medieval England. *Agricultural History Review*, 40.2, 112–26

Blaine, P D, 1858, *An Encyclopaedia of Rural Sports; or a Complete Account ...of Hunting, Shooting, Racing etc*. London. Longman

Bowen, H C, 1975, Aerial archaeology and the development of the landscape in the central parts of southern Britain. In D Wilson (ed), *Aerial Reconnaisance for Archaeology* (= CBA Research Report 12). London. Council for British Archaeology. 103–117

Carr, R, 1976, *English Fox Hunting: A History*. London. Weidenfeld and Nicholson

Crawford, O G S, 1927, Barrows. *Antiquity*, 1, 419–34

Crawford, O G S, and Keiller, A, 1928, *Wessex from the Air*. Oxford. Oxford University Press

Cunliffe, B, 1984, *Danebury: An Iron Age Hillfort in Hampshire*. London. Batsford

Currie, C, 1990, Fish ponds as garden features. *Garden History*, 18.1, 22–33

Currie, C, 1991, The early history of the carp and its economic signicance in England. *Agricultural History Review*, 39, 97–107

Dutt, W A, 1903, *The Norfolk Broads*. London. Methuen

Day, J W, 1954, *History of the Fens*. London. Hartap

Defoe,D, 1724 (reprinted 1971), *A Tour through the whole Island of Great Britain*. Harmondsworth. Penguin

Dyer, C, 1988, The consumption of fish in medieval England. In M Aston (ed), *Medieval Fish, Fisheries and Fish Ponds in England* (= BAR British Series 182). Oxford. British Archaeological Reports. (2 vols.). 27–38

Field, J, 1993, *A History of English Field Names*. London. Longman

Gelling, P, 1977, Excavations at Pilsdon Pen 1964–1971. *Proceedings of the Prehistoric Society*, 43, 263–86

Grant, A, 1988, Animal resources. In G Astill and A Grant (eds), *The Countryside of Medieval England*. Oxford. Basil Blackwell. 149–87

Greenwell, W, 1877, *British Barrows*. London. Clarendon Press

Hadfield, M, 1960, *A History of British Gardening*. Harmondsworth. Penguin

Hansell, P, and Hansell, J, 1988, *Doves and Dovecotes*. Bath. Millstream

Harris, A, and Spratt, D, 1991, The rabbit warrens of the Tabular Hills, North Yorkshire. *Yorkshire Archaeological Journal*, 63, 177–206

Hastings, M, 1969, *Sporting Guns*. London. Longman

Haynes, R G, 1970, Vermin traps and rabbit warrens on Dartmoor. *Post-Medieval Archaeology*, 4, 147–64

Hills, D, and Robertson, P, 1988, *The Pheasant: Management and Conservation*. Oxford. BSP Professional

Hodder, I, 1990, *The Domestication of Europe*. Oxford. Blackwell

Hopkins, H, 1985, *The Long Affray*. London. Secker and Warburg

Hoppitt, R, 1992, *A Study of the Development of Parks in Suffolk from the Early Eleventh Century to the Seventeenth Century*. (Unpublished PhD Thesis, University of East Anglia)

Munsche, P B, 1981, *Gentlemen and Poachers: The English Game Laws 1671–1831*. Cambridge. Cambridge University Press

North, R, 1713, *A Discourse of Fish and Fish Ponds*. London

Orgill, C L, 1936, The introduction of the rabbit into England. *Antiquity*, 10, 462–3

Page, T, 1784, *The Art of Shooting Flying*. London.

Patterson, A, 1909, *Man and Nature on Tidal Waters*. London. Methuen

Payne Galwey, R, 1886, *The Book of Duck Decoys*. London

Prince, H, 1967, *Parks in England*. Isle of Wight. Pinhorn

Rackham, O, 1986, *The History of the Countryside*. London. Dent

RCAHM, 1982, *An Inventory of the Ancient Monuments in Glamorganshire. Volume 1*. Cardiff. HMSO

RCHME, 1975, *An Inventory of the Historical Monuments in the County of Northampton. Volume I. Archaeological Sites in North-East Northamptonshire*. London. HMSO

RCHME, 1982, *An Inventory of the Historical Monuments in the County of Northampton. Volume IV. Archaeological Sites in South-West Northamptonshire*. London. HMSO

Rutledge, P, 1980, A Rabbit Warren at Swainsthorpe. *Norfolk Research Committee Bulletin*, 23, 7

Sheial, J, 1971, *Rabbits and their History*. Newton Abbot. David and Charles

Spencer, H E, 1956, Rabbit. *Transactions of the Suffolk Naturalists Society*, 9, 369

Stamper, P, 1988, Woods and parks. In G Astill and A Grant (eds), *The Countryside of Medieval England*. Oxford. Basil Blackwell. 128–48

Stroud, D, 1965, *Capability Brown*. London. Country Life Books

Switzer, S, 1718, *Ichnographica Rustica*. London. Country Life Books

Taigel, A, and Williamson, T, 1993, *Parks and Gardens*. London. Batsford

Thirsk, J, 1985a, Agricultural policy. In J Thirsk (ed), *The Agrarian History of England and Wales. Volume 2.1. 1640–1750*. Cambridge. Cambridge University Press. 298–388

Thirsk, J, 1985b, Agricultural innovations and their diffusion. In J Thirsk (ed), *The Agrarian History of England and Wales. Volume 2.1. 1640–1750*. Cambridge. Cambridge University Press. 537–587

Thomas, K, 1983, *Man and the Natural World*. London. Allen Lane

Turner, M, 1980, *English Parliamentary Enclosure*. Folkestone. Dawson

Turner, R, 1985, *Capability Brown and the Eighteenth-Century English Landscape*, London. Weidenfeld and Nicholson

Veale, E M, 1957, The rabbit in England. *Agricultural History Review*, 5, 85–90

Warren, H, 1926, Excavations of Pillow Mounds at High Beech, Epping. *Essex Naturalist* 14, 214–26

Whitworth, A, 1993, Yorkshire dovecotes and pigeon lofts: A preliminary survey. *Yorkshire Archaeological Journal*, 65, 75–89

Williams, R, 1987, Rural economy and the antique in the English landscape garden. *Journal of Garden History* 7.1, 73–96

Williamson, T, 1995, *Polite Landscapes: Gardens and Society in Eighteenth-Century England*. London. Alan Sutton

Williamson, T, and Loveday, R, 1988, Rabbits or ritual? Artificial warrens and the Neolithic long mound tradition. *Archaeological Journal*, 145, 290–313

Woodward, E, 1982, *Oxfordshire Parks*. Woodstock. Oxford Museums Service

Zouch, H, 1783, *An Account of the Present Daring Practices of Night-Hunters and Poachers*. London

8   Reflections and postscript

Robert Higham

Reflections

O G S Crawford, a modern pioneer of landscape studies, popularized the 'palimpsest' notion of the landscape, in which the careful observer may disentangle the contributions made by successive generations to our environment, as an historian disentangles the contributions to a manuscript made by successive scribes. This idea of complex and long-evolving landscapes is well illustrated by the papers in this volume.

The study of these landscapes goes back in one sense to the topographers of the sixteenth and seventeenth centuries. As we can see, the subject has much expanded its scope and activity in the present century. Hoskins' *The Making of the English Landscape* set new standards and stimulated much other work. Christopher Taylor's *Dorset* volume, whose 25th publication anniversary is here celebrated, was a prominent example of a series which carried on in the same vein.

Landscape studies is a field which draws much more than a specialist and professional audience of historians, geographers and archaeologists. The understanding of our environment appeals to a broad spectrum of people with local, regional and very much wider interests. One of the very first symposia of Exeter University's Centre for South Western Historical Studies was entitled 'Landscape and Townscape in the South West'; it drew an audience of well over a hundred. The size of the assembly that gathered to hear the papers presented in this volume is further evidence of the continuing widespread appeal of landscapes and their study. In some circles, there is a view that subjects which reach wide audiences have become somehow academically diluted. Nothing could be further from the truth. When something becomes truly 'popular' it is simply further evidence of its importance.

Taking these papers together as a group we find more than the speakers' own subject-matters, there are also some general messages – themes which are either explicit in their remarks or implicit in their material. I would like to pick a few of these out for comment.

First is the plurality and longevity of landscapes and their continuing evolution: they may have ended up as 'The English Landscape', but their development owed much to periods of time long before that notion is relevant. And the result is a fascinating accumulation of present-day, historic, abandoned and buried components.

Second, there are the regional characters of landscapes: these are particularly notable in a country which, for its size, has considerable variety in geological and economic background.

Third, there is the inter-disciplinary approach to landscape studies which, by the very nature of the subject, cannot be avoided: this makes it simultaneously a challenging and rewarding pursuit.

Fourth, there is the need to think not only of the study of landscapes but also of their conservation and management: we must think of landscapes as a precious resource of which we are currently the custodians and which we must pass on to our successors.

Fifth, there are the practical attractions of landscape study as a branch of learning, since it generally depends upon a mixture of library research and what we usually refer to as 'fieldwork'. It enjoys many advantages, being broad-ranging, non-destructive, repeatable and not necessarily expensive. And it can be pursued by committed amateurs as well as by professionals.

Sixth, we have also been reminded in passing, of the contribution which excavation can make to landscape study and of the fact that individually-excavated sites exist not in isolation but as part of wider landscapes. Excavation, of course, can provide specific information on the date and character of occupation which cannot be recovered in any other way, but it is destructive, non-repeatable, site-specific and expensive. And the fact that large-scale excavation is now so difficult to achieve renders even more important the genre of landscape studies under consideration today.

Seventh, and finally, we must remember that landscapes are only partly concrete artefacts and their study is only partly an objective intellectual exercise. Our perceptions of landscapes are always heavily influenced by our own personal and cultural attitudes. Since it is unlikely that we will ever have a complete, objective understanding of how they evolved, we should recognize this more subjective aspect of their study and remember that similarly subjective considerations involving perceptions of space and aesthetics, may have influenced the attitudes of past societies which created and occupied the landscapes we study.

Postscript

In rounding off this collection of papers I find myself coming back to where we started, to Christopher Taylor's publication in 1970 of his county study of Dorset. It was, and remains, a first-class contribution to the field of landscape studies, a simultaneously erudite and readable excursion, one of whose themes was later painted on a wider canvas in his *Village and Farmstead* published in 1983. No more suitable commentator could there have been than he for the 1988 re-issue of Hoskins' pioneering classic *The Making of the English Landscape*.

In the opening chapter of *Dorset* he wrote: 'It is the variety of landscape in Dorset which gives the county its great charm and which has resulted in the equally varied landscape history'. The papers in this volume have been very much an enlargement of that theme, illustrated by a series of studies ranging the length and breadth of England. We are very lucky indeed to have such a rich heritage of landscapes. And lucky also to have a tradition of landscape enquiry to match. As is clear from the discussions, the discipline of landscape history thrives and is still evolving in its methodology and its conceptual framework. These papers mark another, modest, contribution to its development.